BABY RELAX

Y0-BYB-884

BABY RELAX

A PARENT'S GUIDE TO MASSAGE
AND GYMNASTICS FOR CHILDREN

PETER WALKER

Pantheon Books New York

PUBLISHER'S NOTE

As in any such program, the physical benefits to be gained from the exercises in *Baby Relax* can be lost if preexisting conditions are aggravated, so check with your pediatrician before beginning. Also, because the programs are designed to correspond with the growth of an infant, be sure to take care to pace the exercises with that development—be aware of tender soft spots on the head and of the newly healed navel in the infant, and do not force exercises on muscles and joints that are not yet mature enough for them.

Library of Congress Cataloging-in-Publication Data

Walker, Peter, 1942-
Baby relax.

1. Exercise for children. 2. Massage for children. 3. Parent and child. 4. Infants—Care. I. Title.
RJ133.W35   1987   649'.57   86-42973
ISBN 0-394-75171-X

Manufactured in the United States of America

First American Edition

CONTENTS

ACKNOWLEDGMENTS

THANKS TO:

Fiona and Jason

Beatrice and Laura

Christine and Hero

Meg and Christopher

Mary and Graham

Orla and Elliott

Janine and Jack

Marianne and Stephen

Francesca and Portia

Eva and Tyco

Club Sport

Sirens

Roy Victor Studios

Jeb and Michael

FOREWORD

Today, more than ever before, we recognize the role played by physical relaxation and exercise in the pursuit and maintenance of health and fitness. For the very young this role is especially important, as many disorders encountered in childhood, adolescence, and adulthood are known to stem from the stresses, strains, and unresolved traumas that occur in early life. As a practicing osteopath I find that the number of people seeking therapy for muscle and joint disorders and related problems is on the increase. This group includes those who take part in a wide range of popular physical disciplines as well as those leading less active, more sedentary lives, and includes individuals of all ages.

Many of our children who are otherwise healthy display signs of stiff spines, tight hips, tense shoulders, and a variety of postural imbalances related to joints and muscles that have lost or are beginning to lose their flexibility and resilience. Children and adults alike sustain injuries resulting from poor positioning and coordination or from not sensing the strain during physical activity. To some extent this poor sense of body awareness may be due to a lack of movement and of physical contact shortly after birth and during infancy. The continued tightening and contraction of muscles and joints in response to normal and traumatic stress that is experienced by babies may lead to a stiffening up and to postural defects later on in childhood. As the years roll by, this over-stiffening becomes increasingly difficult to counteract: the road from tense abdominal muscles to a stiff backbone is a short one.

Are we doing enough to meet the physical needs of our very young? Should we be taking the structural fitness of our babies and infants more seriously? If we are aware of their tensions, could we be attending to them more effectively? Shouldn't we, once shown the way, do more to actively maintain the healthy function of their muscles and joints, thereby reducing the effects of stress and trauma as they arise and minimizing the possiblity of postural imbalances, structural defects, and injury later on?

This book will help you to help your child take his or her first step in the right direction: a direction that will enhance structural health, assist the development of good posture, and provide a variety of associated benefits. *Baby Relax* will help you to help your child develop strong, supple joints and muscles, and assist his or her ability to withstand all the minor stresses and strains that are so common in early life. It will help to instill body awareness and physical confidence.

The techniques follow and complement all the stages of early development. The author guides you through each stage, and through the transitions from one to the next: from lying to sitting to crawling, standing, and walking. The natural positions will enhance comfort; the massage will soothe and relax, maintain muscle resilience, aid the circulation, and bring a greater sense of physical security. The exercises will preserve and promote flexibility and strength and sow the seeds of good posture.

The methods are gentle, simple, and easy to follow. You will quickly realize that your own natural ability to massage is at your fingertips. The movements used are basic ones. Nothing is forced: the approach is play-oriented, a game.

Peter Walker's workshops clearly demonstrate the joy experienced by babies and parents, the pleasure they receive from the contact and communication. This charming book gives the child-parent relationship a new dimension. It seems obvious that if we are to practice prevention we should start on the ground floor. This book is an investment for your child's health now and for the future.

It is an education to watch Peter Walker at work: his experience and understanding of the physical needs of the very young shine through on these pages. From the osteopathic point of view, this book is of great value: it is as serious in its message and intention as it is delightful in its approach. *Baby Relax* makes a long-awaited and much-needed contribution to infant care—one that extends well into adult life. If we follow its good sense we may well be reducing the number of those in the next generation who are likely to need some forms of treatment.

John Stirk, D.O., M.C.O.

BABY RELAX

INTRODUCTION

Experience, intelligent observation, and documented research prove that the newborn baby is far from devoid of feeling or of reaction to external stimulation. On the contrary, the newborn is an exquisitely sensitive creature that responds both emotionally and physiologically to physical contact and affection.

Physical interaction—movement and touch—is your infant's primary means of self-expression and communication. Its importance is made clear during the first hour of life, when physical contact between a mother and her baby secures the bond of their relationship. For the next eighteen months the child remains extremely body-oriented, while learning to touch, hold, sit, crawl, stand, and walk, and generally to imitate all the movements and activities that he perceives others making.

Physically speaking, this is the most formative time of life, when the infant is most receptive and adaptable. This is the time when, given the right information, parents can nurture in their child a sense of physical security and teach him how to maintain a relaxed and flexible, well-oriented body.

HOLDING AND TOUCHING

At first most parents are anxious about their ability to hold and play with the newborn. Understandably, they regard the child as fragile and delicate, and because of this are inclined to be somewhat wooden in their initial approach. The newborn baby, however, has already received the equivalent of a remarkable massage. Having recovered from being stretched, squeezed, and kneaded from head to foot by the contractions of the mother's womb and birth canal, the baby is supple and resilient.

From this time onwards, various forms of touch, from gentle stroking to firmer rubbing, can be practiced as a natural extension of the parents' desire to nurture and play with their infant. This form of contact baby massage is a constructive embrace that encourages parents and babies to get the "feel" of one another. It engages infants of all ages—the younger the better, as they are then more receptive to it—and it encourages a deeper touch and a more trusting and fulfilling relationship. Babies welcome this kind of affectionate expression: it gives them exactly the stimulation that they need to coordinate their body movements. Also, it is made easy by the fact that the newborn baby remains mostly in one of three basic positions: on his back, side, or stomach.

Baby massage is a panacea, a remedy for many of the minor ills of childhood. Its soothing, calming effect makes it an ideal way of enhancing a child's sleep and thereby increasing all the benefits of relaxation. It can relieve tension, pacify trauma, and ease the mild digestive disorders that are common in early infancy.

Baby massage is an ideal introduction to baby gymnastics. This is a gentle mode of play that makes full use of the child's remarkable range of movement to ensure the strengthening of a flexible and well coordinated body.

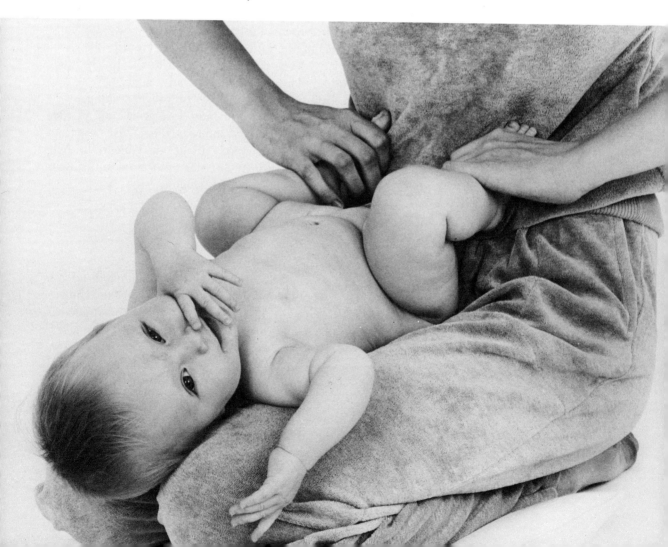

MASSAGE AND MOVEMENT

Within the first two to three months of life the infant becomes more fully oriented to her new world. At birth she emerges from the squat fetal position, uncurls herself, lifts her head slightly, straightens her spine, and stretches her muscles to open out the body's joints. This is the time when parents can sow a seed of health and fitness for their child. Practiced at this time, a baby exercise program promotes the infant's physical attributes of relaxed strength and flexibility. It encourages a more satisfying child-parent relationship and helps fulfill the infant's need for movement and contact.

Baby gymnastics familiarizes parents with their infants' range of movement and gives them a means of checking to ensure that the bumps and falls so prevalent in early childhood have no lasting repercussions upon their children's flexibility. The young infant is courageous and adventurous, and has a natural urge to explore the potential activity that accompanies each phase of her development. With baby gymnastics, parents may safely encourage this attiude, having established trust and faith in their child's capabilities.

Baby massage and baby gymnastics are both therapeutic forms of play oriented towards securing health and fitness with relaxation—and relaxation in action. They will provide the parent with a means of fulfilling the infant's everyday physical needs and allow the infant the opportunity to fulfill her own physical aspirations. Baby massage and baby gymnastics are not things you do *to* a child; they are things you do *with* a child. They become richly rewarding games of communication when practiced with the full cooperation of the child and a loving touch.

YOUR BABY'S PHYSICAL DEVELOPMENT

Throughout the world, children of all cultures follow an identical pattern of development. Every child has the same primitive reflex movements, and every child loses these reflex movements as controlled movement begins. Every child stretches as he strengthens, and strengthens from the head downwards, coordinating the head and neck before the arms and shoulders, and the arms and shoulders before the legs and feet. Most children sit before crawling properly and crawl before standing and walking.

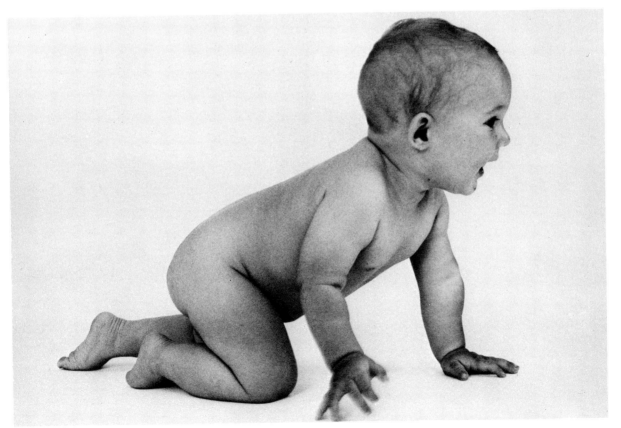

Your infant's development is a continual progression involving the acquisition of one faculty after another, and no amount of persuasion can make your child learn a relevant skill until his nervous system acknowledges that he is emotionally and physically capable. This order of development is a natural instinctive pattern, and you have no influence over its sequence; nor should you hurry your child through a sequence. Some children sit late and crawl early, while others crawl early and stand late, and so on. The child needs to acquaint himself fully with each sequence before moving on to the next. And as with all living and growing things, your baby will flourish if given a good environment with proper guidance and loving care.

The newborn baby feels, sees, hears, tastes, as well as sucks and swallows. He sleeps for much of the time, lying in one or more of the three basic positions:

On the back.

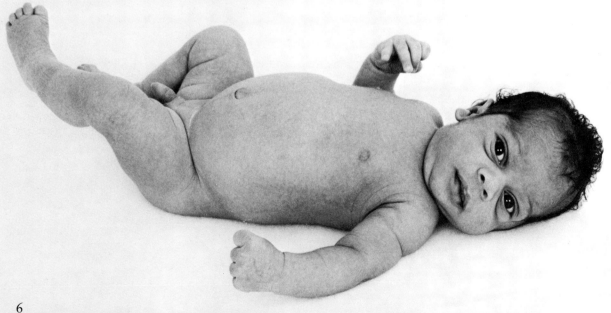

On the side.

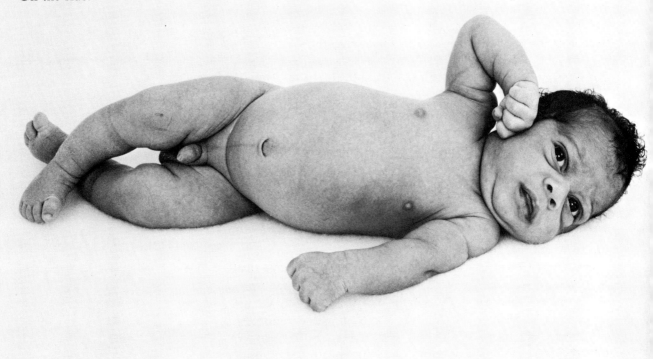

On the belly.

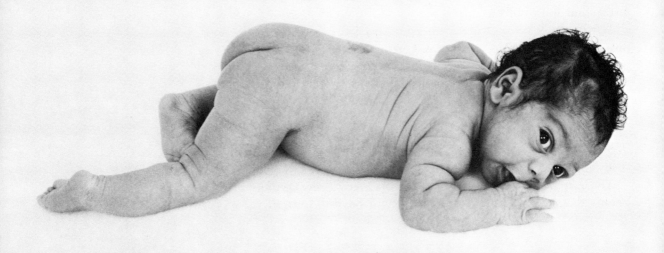

Whatever position your baby finds most comfortable is the best, but there are distinct advantages to placing your baby on his belly. Firstly, this means that the infant's entire body—head, trunk, arms, legs, hands, and feet—are in contact with the surface he is lying on. Secondly, this position is secure and calming, and ensures that regurgitated milk cannot flow back into the baby's throat. Thirdly, it soothes the digestive organs by gently stretching and relaxing the abdominal muscles.

The belly position is in harmony with your baby's development as it encourages him to lift his head and gain strength in the back of the neck and spine, and develops the flexibility of the spine. As your child spends so much time in a resting position it is essential that you allow him to rest in the position he finds most comfortable. But laying your baby on his side for a few minutes at a time before placing him on his belly may make it easier for him to accept this position.

The newborn baby is capable of a variety of movements that she makes in response to specific stimulation. These responses, termed *reflexes*, play a major part in the survival of the very young baby and in establishing the child's relationship with her mother. The reflex movements of the newborn give way to voluntary movements as the infant develops, and this usually takes some months. Many of the baby's reflex movements are obvious: for example, when the baby's cheek comes in contact with the mother's breast, instinctively the head turns towards it, and she sucks when her mouth is stimulated with the nipple. When touched and stroked around the palms of the hands and the soles of the feet she instinctively clasps her hands and curls her toes. This reaction can be a means of allowing the baby to secure herself to her mother when being held or carried. When startled, the young baby instinctively throws open her limbs and then draws them back in again as if attempting to embrace her mother for protection and comfort.

When a very young baby is placed on her belly, she lifts and turns her head. This movement, also instinctive, ensures that the newborn baby can breathe freely in this position. When a newborn is held standing, she walks instinctively. The baby has a number of other reflex movements, some of which are designed as a form of self-defense. Unlike most adults and other children, babies also show a great deal of general activity in response to pleasure: their respiration increases, their eyes open wide, and they move their arms and legs about vigorously.

The fact that the newborn employs so many reflex actions means that her movements are inclined to be stiff and jerky.

Massaging your baby at this time can also assist her body coordination, and as the infant relaxes, her movements become smoother.

Between about three and seven months, when lying on his belly the baby will push his arms and hands in front of his body for support while trying to take a good look around. As his neck and upper back begin to grow stronger, the baby will lift his head higher, and as his arms grow stronger he will lift his chest and shoulders from the floor. The baby's head control will now improve so that when held in a sitting position he will not bob from side to side but remain sturdy, and when lying on his belly the baby will now raise and turn his head from side to side in order to take in more of his environment.

At about this time your baby will quickly learn how to sway his body from side to side and make use of his ability to roll his head to gain the momentum required to roll his body over. Take care not to leave your child unattended on high surfaces.

Once your baby has developed this degree of strength and coordination in the upper back, neck, and head, he should be ready to try supported sitting positions.

The first position ensures that your baby's legs are properly aligned with the trunk at the hip joints. It will maintain the flexibility of your child's hips and knees and is highly complementary to this phase of development. This position will give your baby the opportunity to push himself into a sitting position unaided and in his own time. In addition, it will encourage the strengthening of your baby's hands, arms, shoulders, back, and spine.

Sitting comfortably with your legs in front of you, lay your baby on your thighs. Talk and sing to and soothe your baby, and gently sway your knees from side to side. Now open your baby's knees and bring the soles of his feet together.

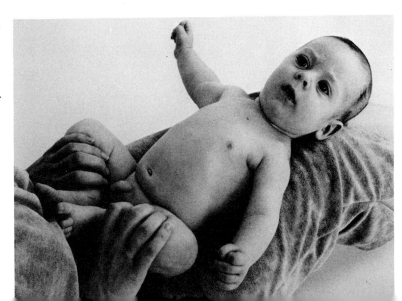

Now lift your knees to sit your
baby more upright.

Now lift your knees even more
and sit your baby upright.

Practice this until your baby is
able to sit comfortably when
supported, and then try
supporting your child from
behind, in the same position, on
the floor.

Encourage your baby to lean forward onto his hands. Play with your child in this position for as long as he will allow. When this is comfortable, sit your baby in the same position, leaning forward onto a cushion and supported by a cushion on each side to prevent him from rolling sideways.

Play with your baby in this position, and gradually increase the time spent in the position by a minute or two until your baby is able to sit unaided in this "tailor" pose.

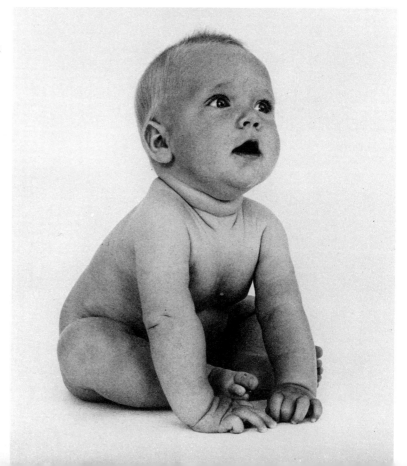

The second sitting position is with your child sitting between his feet. This position maintains the flexibility of the knees and ankles and assists crawling. This should be encouraged once your child has achieved the "tailor" pose.

With your baby lying belly forward upon your thighs, talk and sing to soothe your baby, gently swaying your knees from side to side. Turn both your baby's feet inwards, with the insteps towards the buttocks.

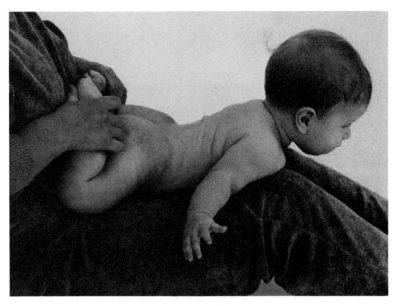

Now encourage your baby to sit upright.

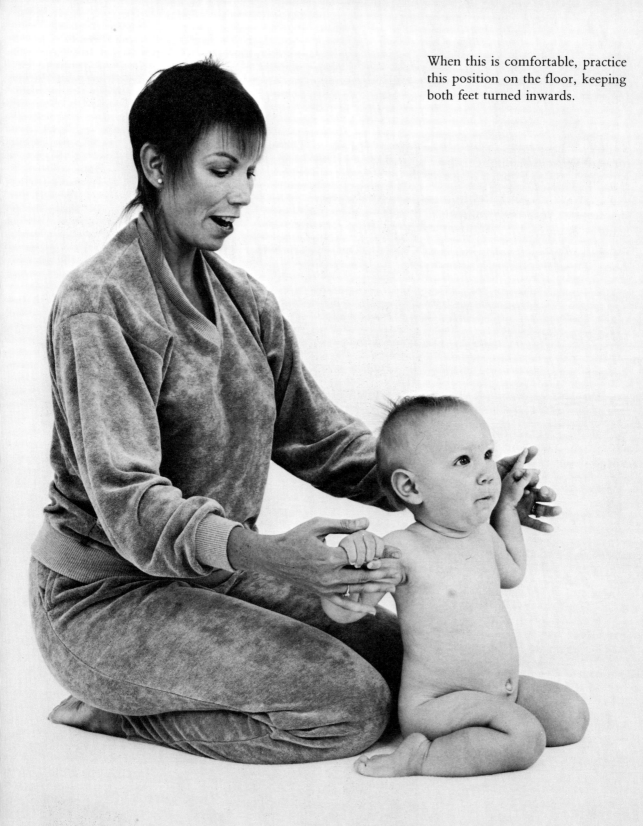

When this is comfortable, practice
this position on the floor, keeping
both feet turned inwards.

14

Play with your baby in this position, and gradually increase the amount of time spent on this exercise until your child is able to sit upright unaided. Do not leave your baby unattended in this position until he is completely comfortable in it.

From about seven to twelve months your baby will begin to crawl. The timing of this varies greatly, as some babies crawl earlier than others and some hardly crawl at all in a recognizable fashion. Styles of crawling include a diagonal shuffle across the floor, crawling backwards, pulling the whole body forwards while trailing the legs, and rocking backwards and forwards on all fours.

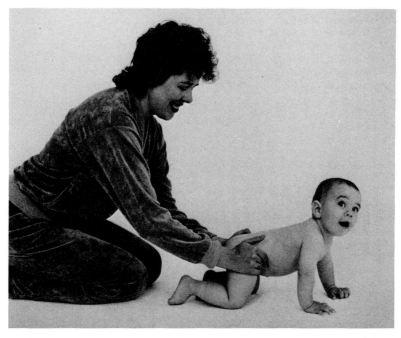

Supported sitting between the feet encourages crawling, and from this position you can encourage your child to lean forward . . .

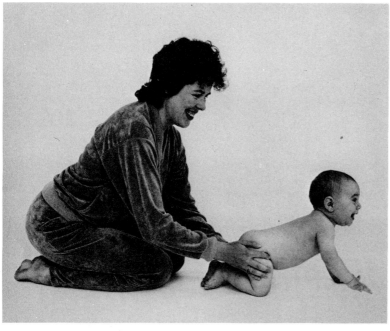

and then to return her buttocks back onto her feet. Play with your baby in this position and repeat as often as she allows.

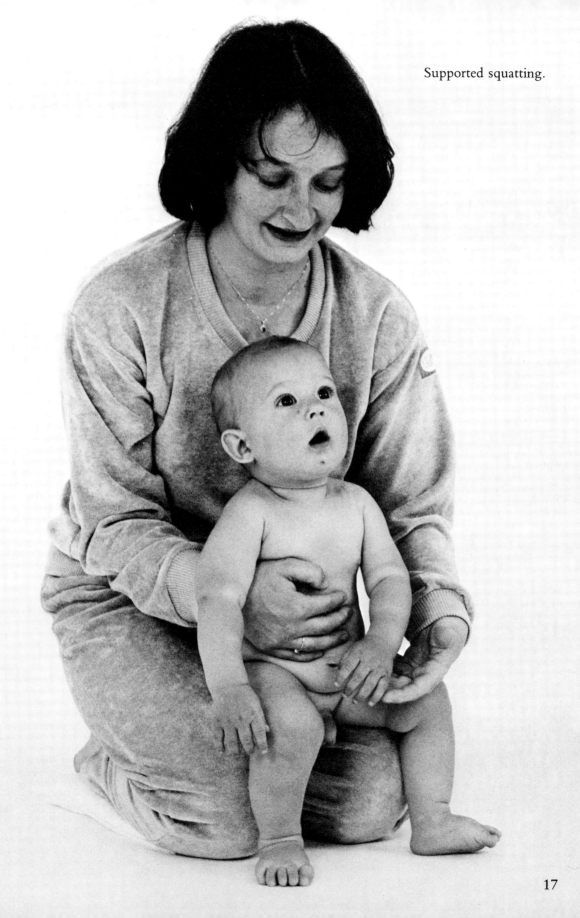

Supported squatting.

To all fours.

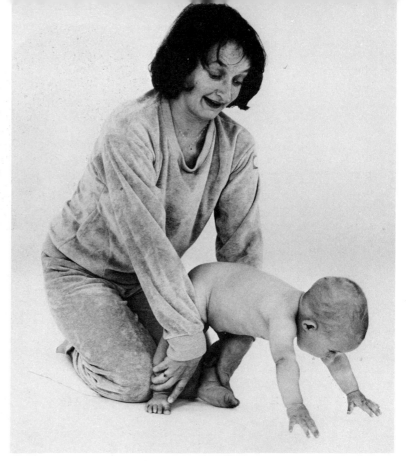

This strengthens the legs and also encourages crawling.

As the child's legs become stronger she will start to pull herself up and stand supported.

Between twelve and eighteen months the child is able to stand supported, and in excitement bobs up and down. This movement also stengthens the legs for standing, and she can be encouraged from squatting . . .

to standing.

Holding your child securely by the hips keeping both feet firmly on the floor encourages standing.

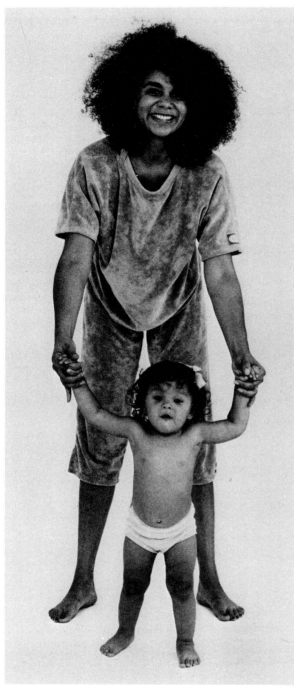

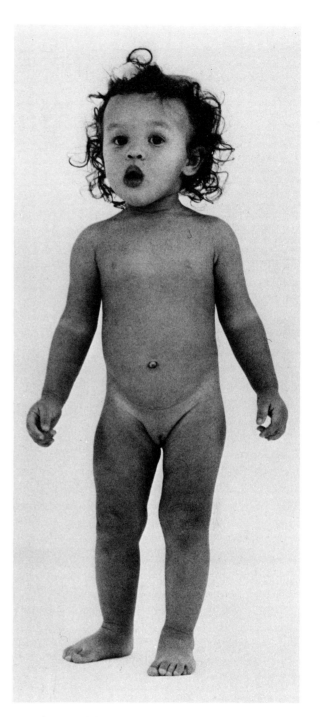

And holding the child's hands from behind, making sure that your child takes her own weight, and leads, encourages walking.

Standing and holding onto furniture increases the child's skill and confidence. Leaving suitable furniture within reach will encourage a child to take her first tentative steps.

A THERAPEUTIC TOUCH

In 1956 Marcelle Geber, on a research grant from the United Nations Children's Fund, traveled to Africa to study child intelligence in the Third World. While in Uganda, she made a startling discovery: there she found "the most precocious, brilliant, and advanced infants ever observed anywhere." These children were welcomed into the world and treated with love, care, concern, and gentleness. Born at home, they slept and fed according to the rhythm of their needs and remained constantly with their mothers, who massaged them, sang to them, and continually fondled and caressed them. Within the first few days of life these babies, "held only by their forearms, sat upright with beautiful straight backs, perfect head balance, and finely focused eyes, smiling at their mothers."

They were alert, happy, watchful, and calm. They smiled rapturously, and all three hundred of the infants observed "crawled skillfully and sat upright unsupported at six to seven weeks of age." Further observation showed that up to the age of four, all these babies were physically and intellectually far in advance of their European counterparts. When the child reaches the age of four, however, according to the traditions of that culture the mother breaks the maternal bond: she "carefully, completely, and without any forewarning, totally abandons her child . . . she suddenly refuses even to acknowledge the child's existence . . . the child is then sent to a distant village to be raised by relatives or given to neighbors." From this point on, the bond with the mother having been broken, the phenomenal pace of the child's development ceased.

Developments in the field of psychiatry and psychology reveal the birth experience and the period of sensitivity immediately following it as being of great significance to the individual's general approach to life. Such observations might imply that when a child is born without unnecessary trauma and is received with loving care, she retains a sense of her own capability and a trust in the world as something benevolent that is continuing to meet her needs. This powerful first impression can reduce the level of alienation and despair felt by the individual and can endow him or her with an ability to cope with new and stressful situations. It can contribute greatly towards the body's capacity to prevent and heal its illnesses.

More recent research shows that during pregnancy the fetus shares and is affected physiologically by its mother's emotions; it prepares for birth and together with the mother initiates labor, and having done so, is adequately prepared for the intricate series of turns that it needs for negotiating the birth canal.

Given the appropriate conditions, birth can be seen as a perfectly coordinated series of movements in which a relaxed and prepared mother and child move spontaneously together step by step through a fundamental natural process.

Labor is recognized as having three phases. During the first, the contracting womb presses against the child's body, pushing it downwards until the head lies secure within the opening of the birth canal. In the second, the baby is kneaded and squeezed through the birth canal in order to enter the world. These first two phases of birth are actually equivalent to a massage that kneads and squeezes the infant's body from head to toe. This stimulates the newborn's major internal organs and glands.

The third and final phase of birth is the release of the placenta. At this time the umbilical connection is replaced by the bond of affection that arises through parent–child recognition and their physical contact with each other.

From birth onwards baby massage presents an ideal opportunity for you and your new baby to "get the feel of each other," to establish close physical contact and soothe away any tensions that may have arisen as a result of the birth experience. It is now known that even premature babies, some weighing less than two pounds, benefit from massage and respond by purring and stretching. Recent medical observations confirm that when baby massage forms part of an important program designed to counteract the adverse effects of a premature birth, it improves the child's responses to the mother, encourages tranquility, and hastens weight gain and physical development.

From India to Africa and to the Arctic, massage is still included as a spontaneous and vital part of the relationship between parents and their children. These mothers massage their infants frequently while nursing, and in certain cultures every baby is given a ceremonial massage shortly after birth.

A RELAXED APPROACH

Massage is a natural activity that we all perform at some time or other, probably daily, without giving the matter further consideration. It is the spontaneous rubbing and kneading of the muscles, bones, and joints to release and relieve them of aches, pains, and tensions. It is a natural way of restoring or increasing the pleasurable sensations that emanate from the human body.

Learning to massage your baby is a practical expression of your love and care. It is an extremely useful art. Easy, and mostly intuitive, it is as beneficial as it is joyful. Time spent massaging your baby is time spent getting to know your baby, getting to know how your child likes to be touched and where. Some infants love having their bellies rubbed; others love having their backs stroked, their heads tickled, and so on.

PREPARATION

Before you begin to massage your baby, make sure that your hands are clean, that your fingernails do not overlap the ends of your fingers, and that you yourself are relaxed. A few minutes' initial preparation is well worth while, as it will release any excessive tension in your shoulders, arms, and hands, and will prevent you from transferring it to your child.

To assist your relaxation, just sit up straight for a few moments and check that your belly is relaxed. Also make sure that your chest and belly are working in harmony, expanding together with each inhalation and contracting together with each exhalation. Now pull your shoulders downwards and backwards, pulling your shoulder blades together. Repeat this process four or five times. Now massage a little oil onto your hands and warm them by rubbing them briskly together. Interlock your fingers and straighten them. Now sit up straight, pull your shoulder blades together, and, relaxing your hands from your wrists, shake them several times.

WHEN?

When to massage your child depends upon your own mood and your baby's response. It can be done before or after changing diapers, feeding, or bathing, before sleeping, or if you are just sitting with your infant with no particular objective in mind other than to enjoy each other's company.

WHERE?

Where you massage your child depends upon your baby's response and disposition. Massaging the head and back is generally soothing. Massaging the arms and hands, legs and feet, generally proves warming and relaxing; or, if you have someting specific in mind, massaging the belly aids digestion and massaging the chest aids respiration. Massage can include any or all parts of the body and should be practiced whenever you both enjoy it.

HOW?

To find out what brings forth the most joyful response from your baby, variations of touch can be explored in the following order. First, *effleurage:* a light movement using the fingers or the whole hand to stroke the surface of your baby's skin. Second, *rubbing:* a more penetrative movement that uses the weight of relaxed hands to feel the contours of the child's muscles. Finally, *kneading:* using the whole hand to gently squeeze and rub the muscles to encourage their relaxation.

STAY RELAXED

Try to adopt a position that will allow you to sustain a state of relaxation for a reasonable period of time. One comfortable position is to sit with your legs in front of you and with your head, upper back, and shoulders supported. Support the small of your back with a cushion, and lift your knees.

In this position you can support your child comfortably upon your thighs so as to maintain body contact and leave your hands free. If necessary, you can place another cushion under your knees.

When massaging your baby, take your time: there is no hurry; you can do it as little or as often as you like. Find out where your baby likes to be stroked; start from there, and slowly add to your routine. In this way you will soon become adept and confident in handling and massaging your baby.

BABY MASSAGE

At birth the newborn baby is subjected to an extreme drop in the temperature of her environment. This is a sudden decrease of at least twenty-five degrees, the temperature of the mother's womb being around 98°F, and that of a warm room at around 73°F. What is more, the infant's organs of circulation are not yet fully functional, causing the child to experience a loss of body heat four times more rapid than that of any normal adult.

The newborn is usually protected to some extent by a coat of vernix, and this oily second skin insulates and protects the baby from the effects of a lengthy exposure to the liquid environment of the womb. The vernix provides a natural source of insulation; its properties are highly nutritious, and are mostly absorbed through the surface of the infant's skin a few hours after the birth.

During the days that you and your baby are resting together, recovering from the labor and the experience of birth, you can begin to introduce massage by stroking or gently kneading your baby with the aid of a pure oil. This oil will replace the insulating coat of vernix and help your child to retain body warmth. It will stimulate your child's circulation, an inner source of warmth and nutrition, and generate relaxation and heat through contact and friction.

From this time on the following techniques can be used to guide your intuition. With your baby lying on your thighs, talk and sing to her, soothe and relax her by gently swaying your legs from side to side.

ARMS AND LEGS

Place your hands on your baby's
shoulders.

Now, gently and slowly, using the weight of your relaxed hands, draw your hands over the shoulders.

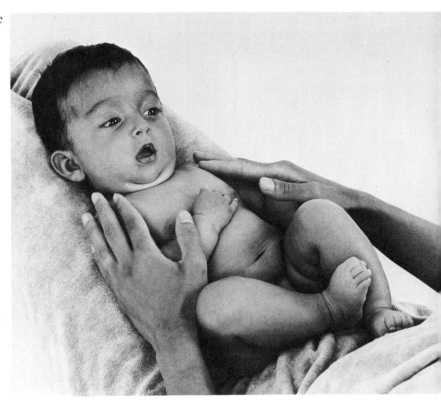

And down the arms.

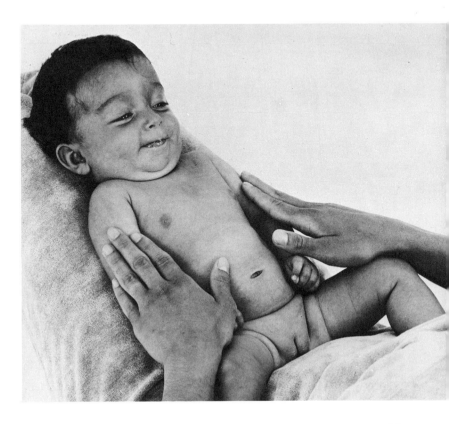

Repeat until your baby relaxes
and straightens her arms. Now,
holding her forearm with one
hand, gently stroke down the arm
with the other.

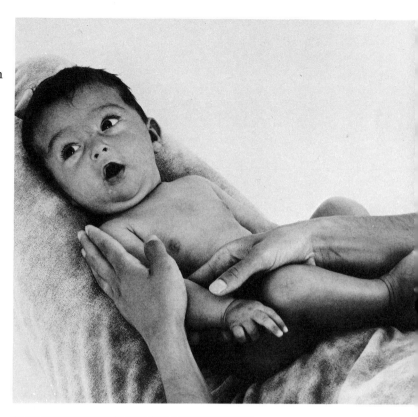

Now, using fingertip pressure,
massage the ridge in the center of
the forearm from the wrist to the
elbow.

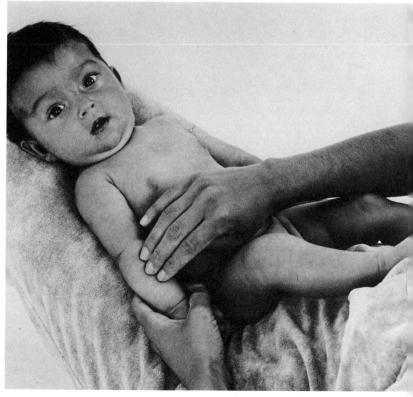

Gently knead the sides and inside of the forearm with your thumbs.

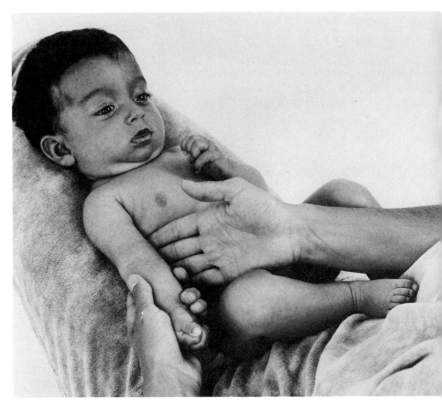

Gently knead the upper arm, squeezing with your whole hand.

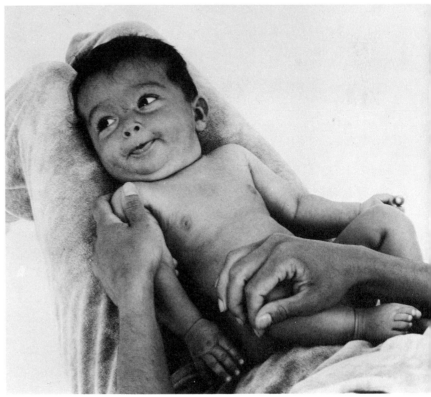

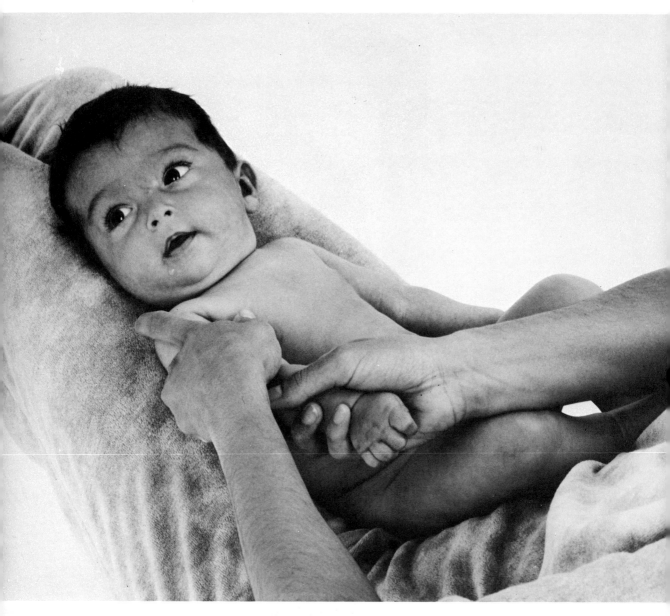

Now, to complete the massage,
hold her arm gently with both
hands and pull the whole arm and
hand gently through the palms of
your hands.

Repeat (for both arms) all or any of
these movements as often as is
pleasurable.

Using fingertip pressure, gently massage along the ridge of the shin bone, from the knee to the ankle.

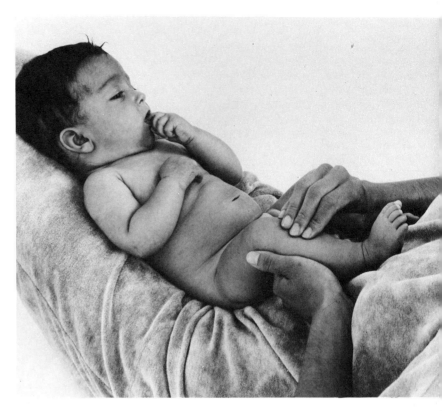

Now massage the front muscle of the lower leg, gently kneading with your thumb.

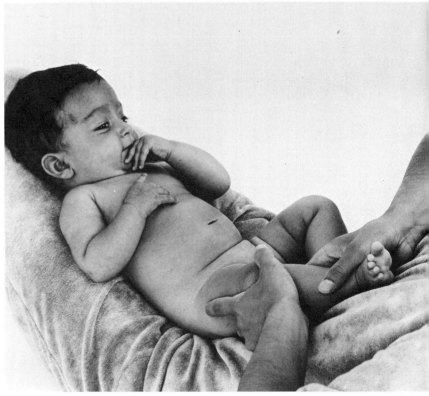

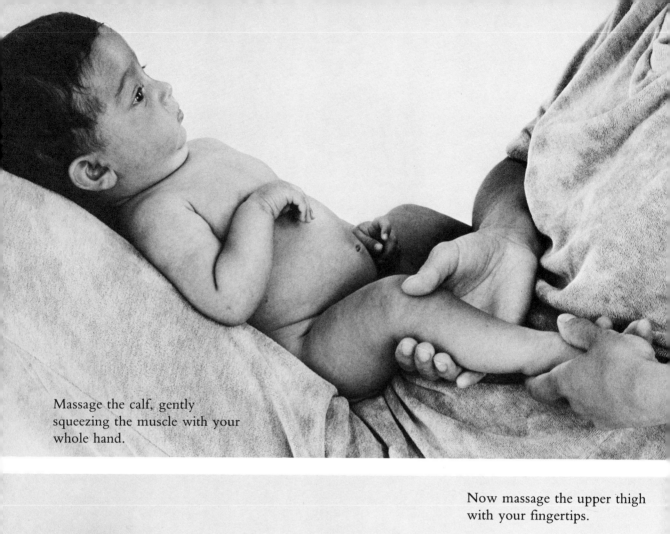

Massage the calf, gently
squeezing the muscle with your
whole hand.

Now massage the upper thigh
with your fingertips.

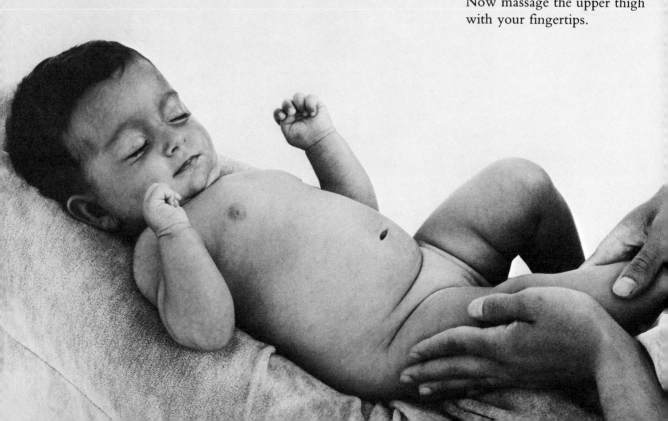

Massage the front of the thigh, kneading gently with your whole hand.

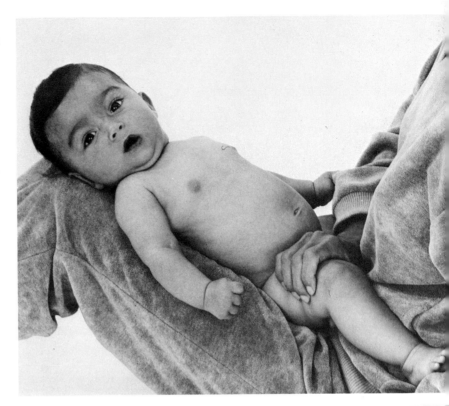

Now the back of the thigh, kneading and squeezing gently with your whole hand.

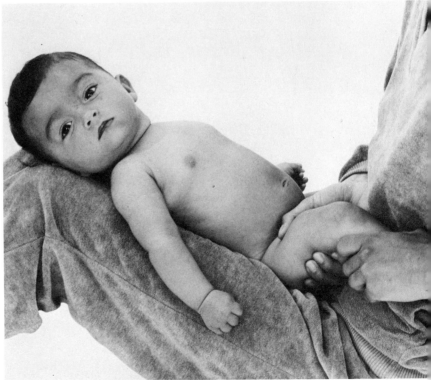

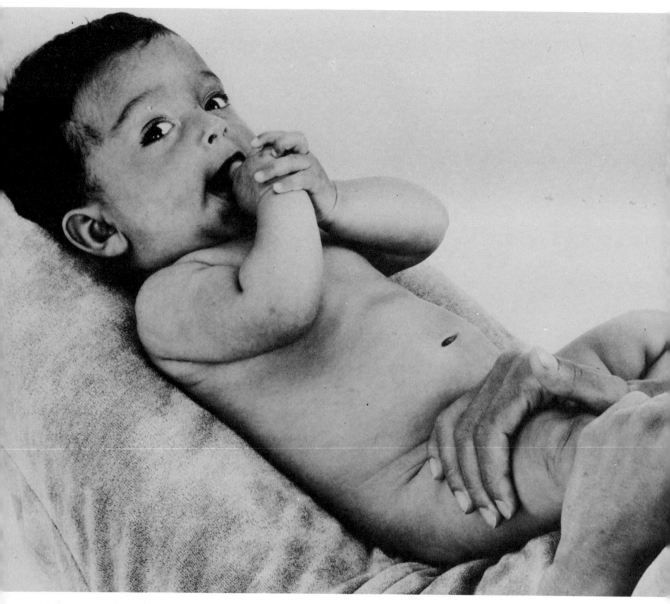

Now complete the massage by
pulling the leg and foot through
the palms of your hands. Repeat
for both legs and feet.

Repeat as often as is pleasurable.

HANDS AND FEET

Because the infant's circulation is not fully developed, the baby's extremities—hands and feet—are usually several degrees cooler than the rest of the body. Most young babies keep their feet and toes curled inwards and their hands and fingers clenched. Massaging the hands and the feet promotes warmth and relaxation throughout the entire body and stimulates the circulation. It is an unobtrusive form of massage that is relaxing and refreshing and especially useful during sensitive periods such as early teething.

According to reflexology, an ancient system of massage, areas of the hands and feet are connected through the nervous system of the body's various internal organs. Reflexologists maintain that the stimulation of these areas through massage has a highly beneficial effect upon the functioning of these organs.

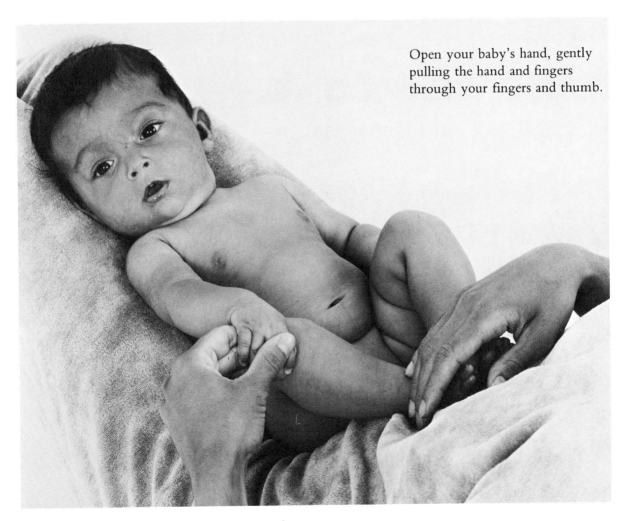

Open your baby's hand, gently pulling the hand and fingers through your fingers and thumb.

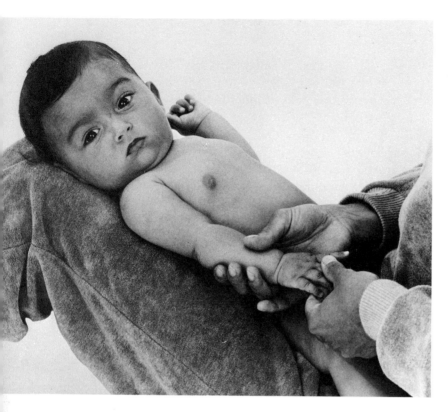

Gently feel the structure of the hand, and with your thumb and forefinger, press and roll each finger.

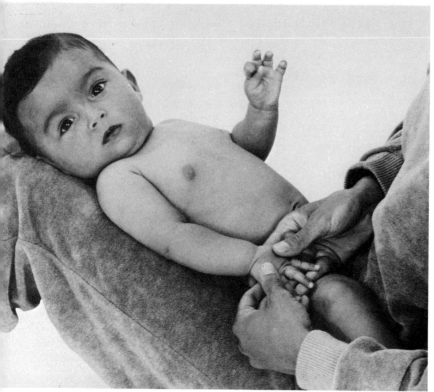

Open the fingers like a fan.

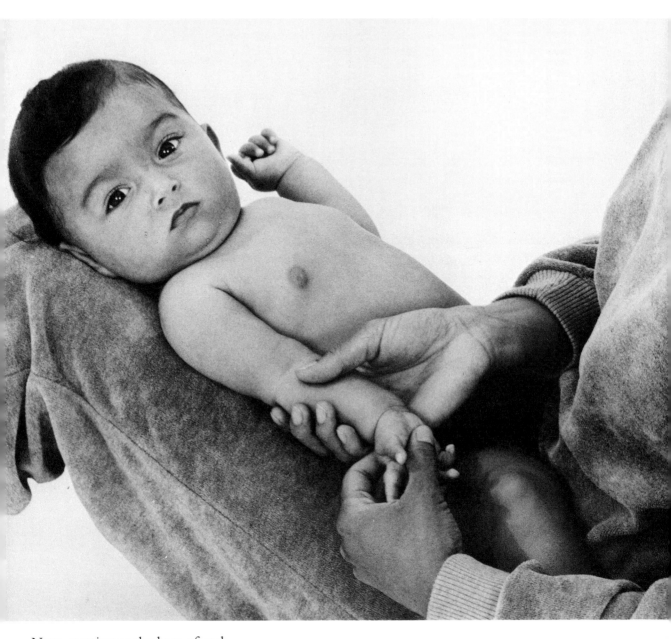

Now, starting at the base of each
finger, press each joint and gently
press and roll with your finger and
thumb from the periphery to the
center of the palm.

Repeat for both hands.

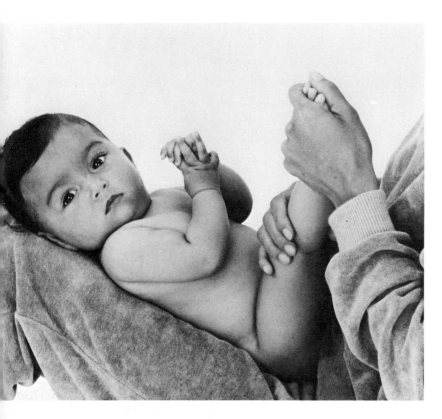

Open your baby's foot by gently pulling the foot through your fingers and thumb.

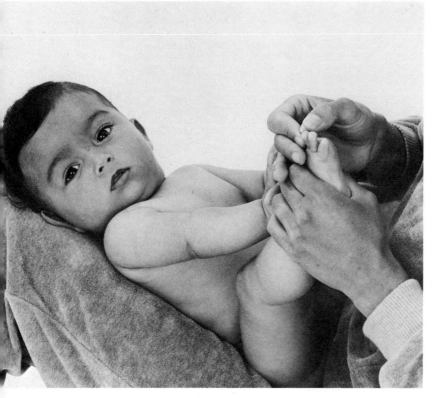

Gently feel the structure of the foot, and press and roll each toe with your thumb and forefinger.

Open the toes like a fan.

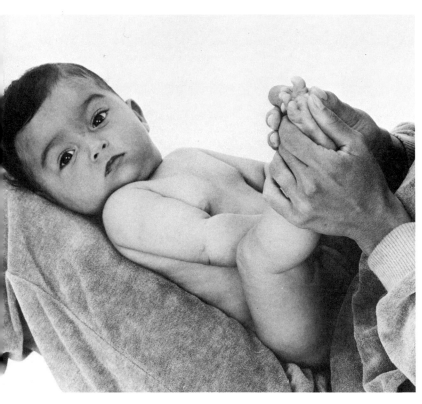

Now, starting from the base of each toe, gently press and roll with your thumb and forefinger, and massage the sole of the foot.

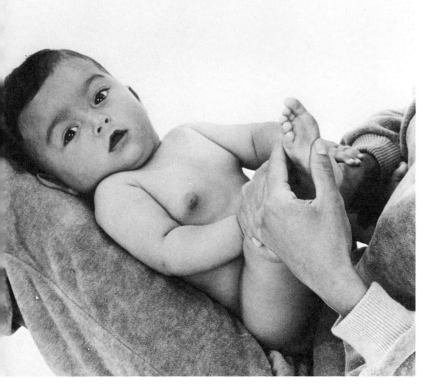

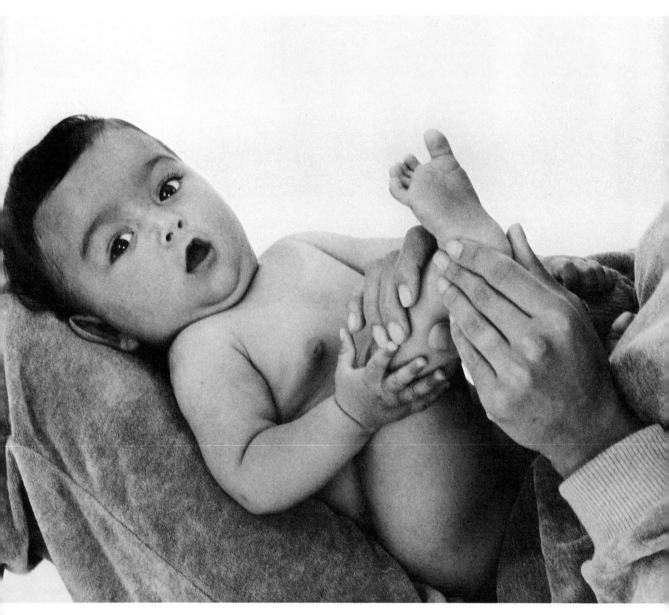

Now press gently all around the
heel bone, rolling with your
thumb and forefinger.

SHOULDERS, CHEST, AND BELLY

Massage around the tips of the shoulders, kneading and squeezing gently with your fingers and thumbs.

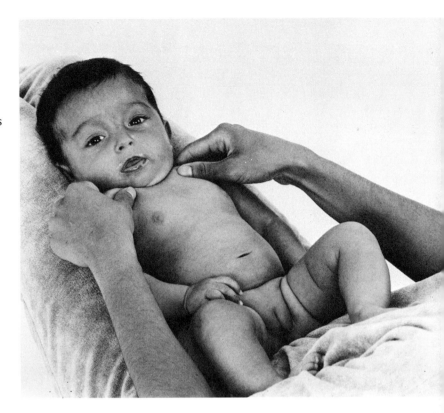

Now place your hands on the upper chest with your fingers curled over the shoulders, and squeeze and knead gently, using your whole hand, being careful not to irritate the child's breasts, which are sensitive during her breast-fed phase.

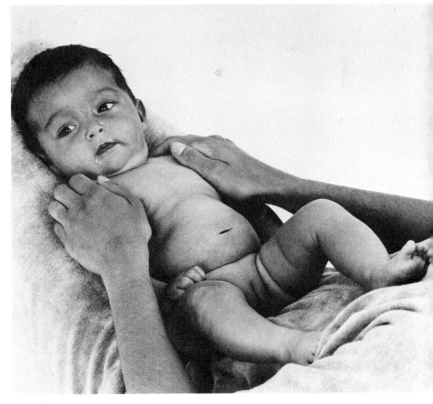

Now place your fingers on the
center of the upper chest . . .

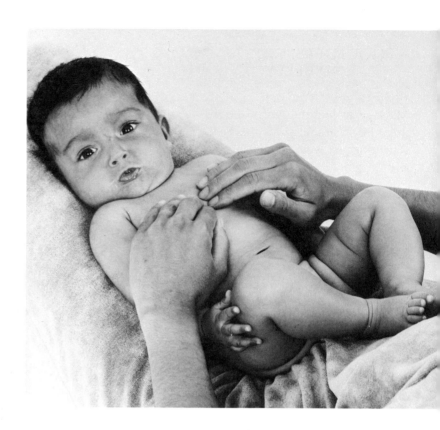

and gently massage upwards and
outwards over the shoulders.

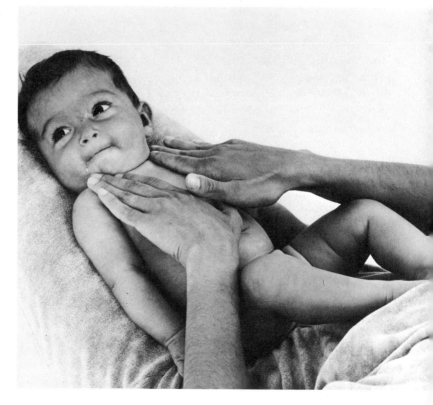

Now place your fingers on the
center of the lower chest . . .

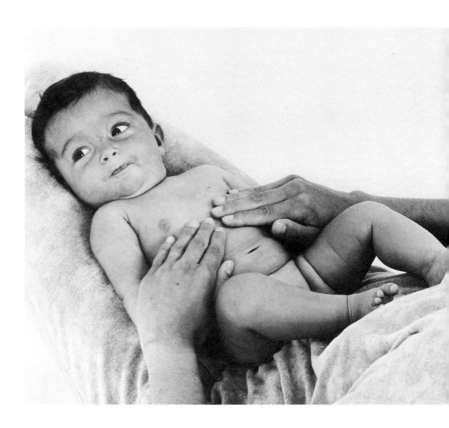

and gently massage downwards
and outwards in the same
direction as the ribs.

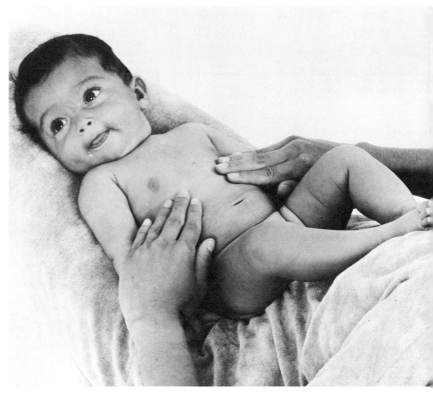

Now gently place both your
hands on your baby's chest and
draw them outwards over the
arms.

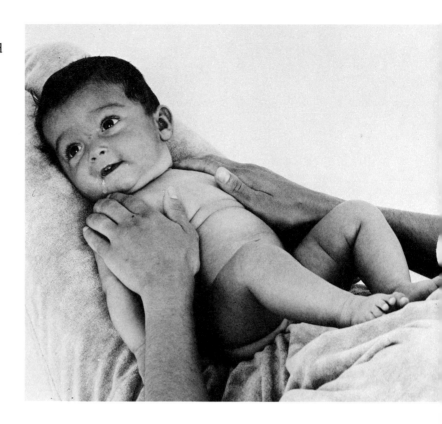

Gently lay your hand across your
baby's belly. Squeeze very gently
and move your hand gently from
side to side.

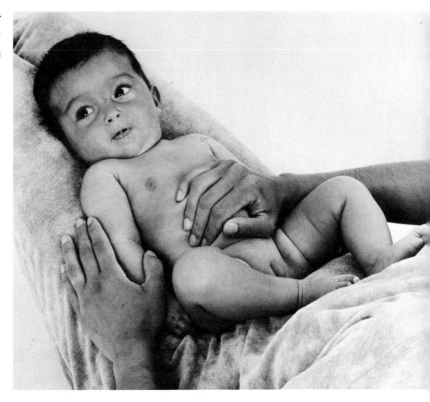

Lay your relaxed hands, one
above the other, across your
baby's belly, and move them
gently clockwise around the
navel, taking care to maintain
contact with one hand by lifting
the other as you complete each
circular movement.

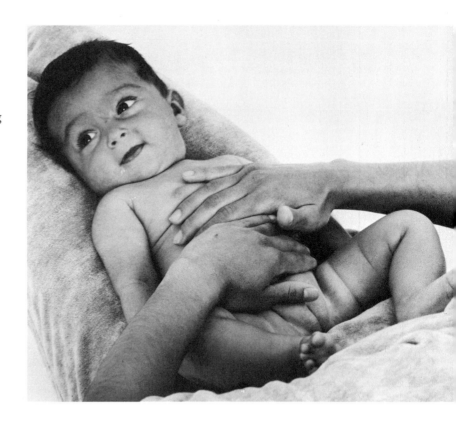

Repeat the same clockwise
movement around the navel with
gentle fingertip pressure of both
hands.

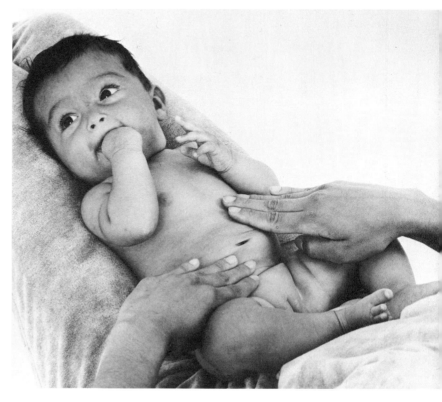

Repeat the same movement using
the gentle fingertip pressure of
one hand, moving around the
navel in widening circles.

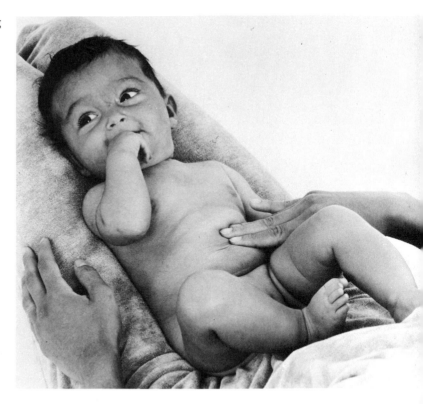

Repeat again, using the relaxed
weight of both hands.

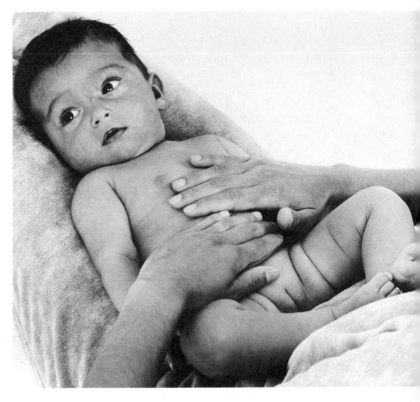

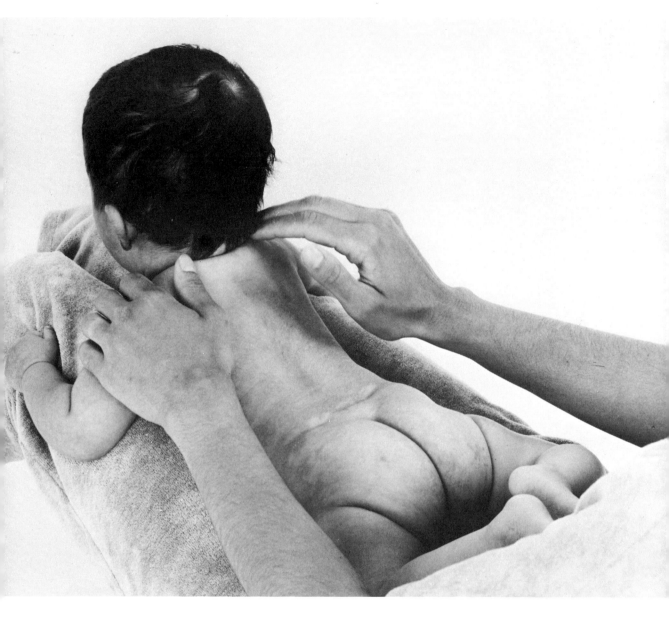

BACK

Lay your baby on her belly on your thighs. Talk and sing to her, stroke and soothe her, allowing your knees to sway gently from side to side. Place your relaxed hands, with the fingers curled, over the top of your baby's shoulders.

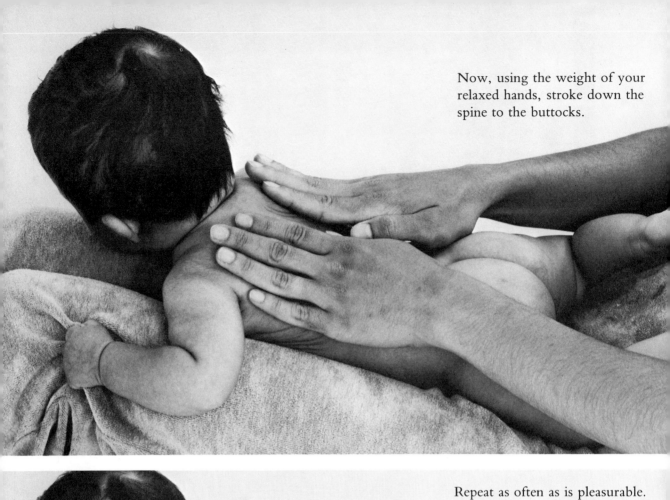

Now, using the weight of your relaxed hands, stroke down the spine to the buttocks.

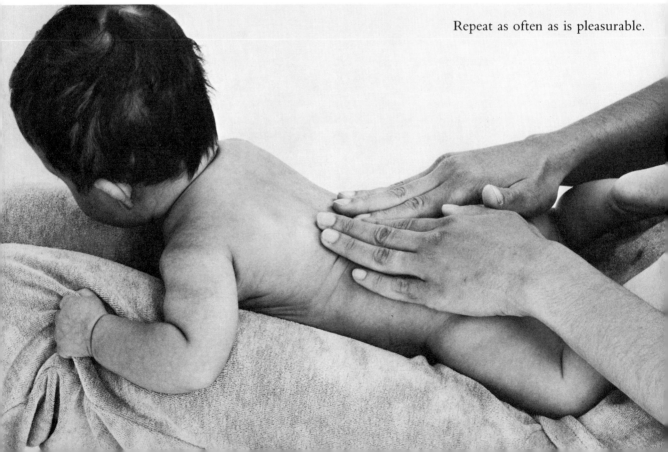

Repeat as often as is pleasurable.

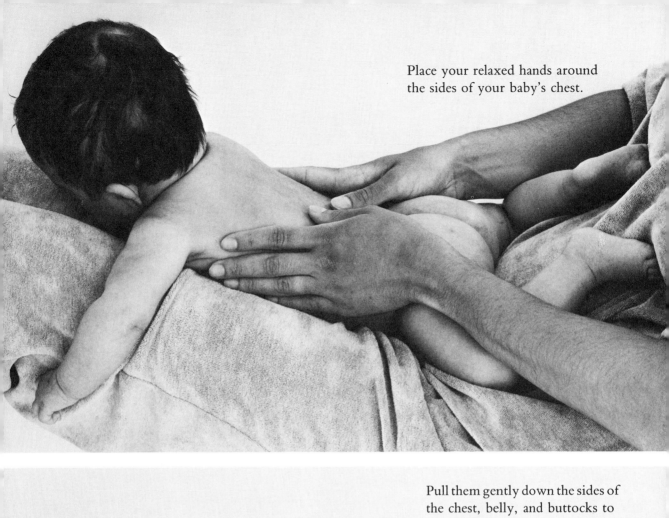

Place your relaxed hands around the sides of your baby's chest.

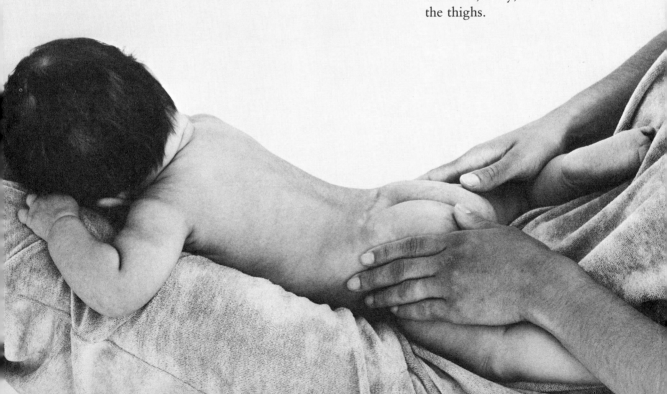

Pull them gently down the sides of the chest, belly, and buttocks to the thighs.

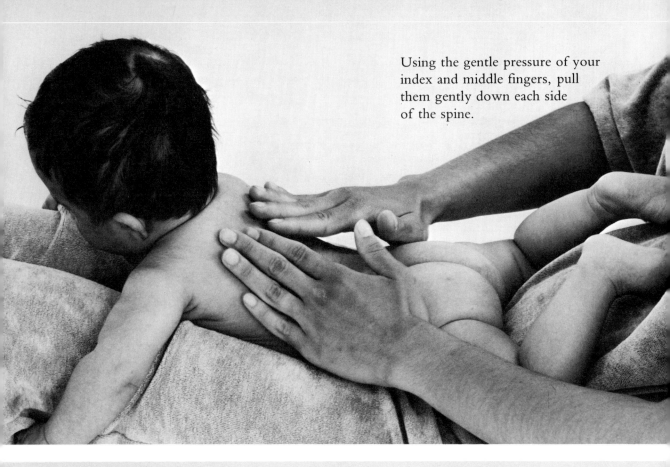

Using the gentle pressure of your index and middle fingers, pull them gently down each side of the spine.

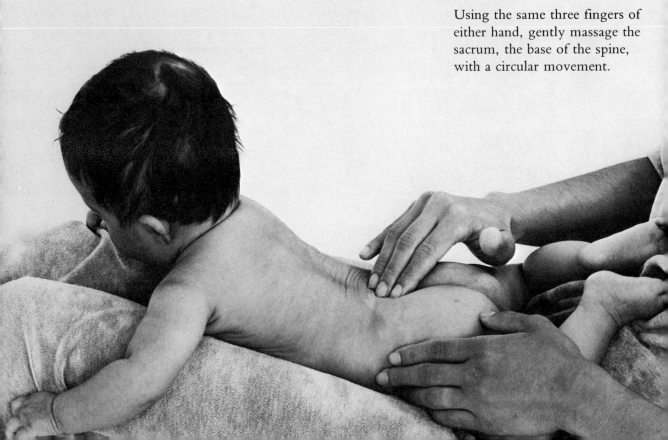

Using the same three fingers of either hand, gently massage the sacrum, the base of the spine, with a circular movement.

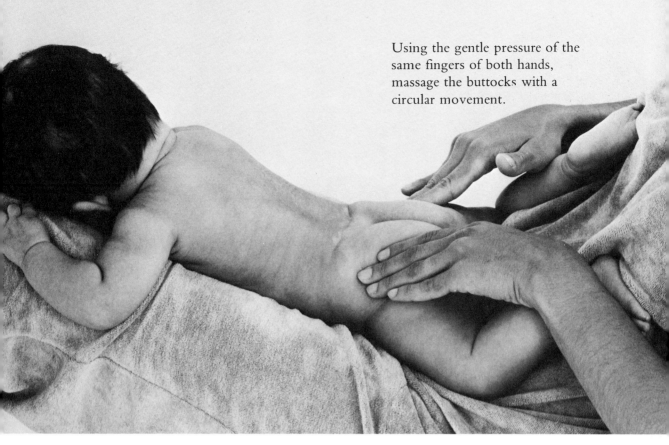

Using the gentle pressure of the same fingers of both hands, massage the buttocks with a circular movement.

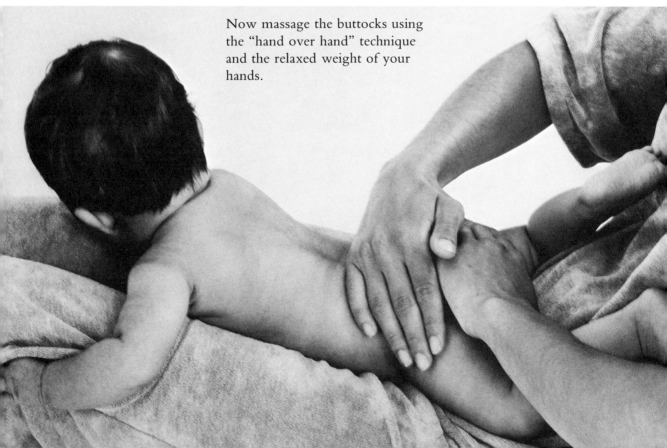

Now massage the buttocks using the "hand over hand" technique and the relaxed weight of your hands.

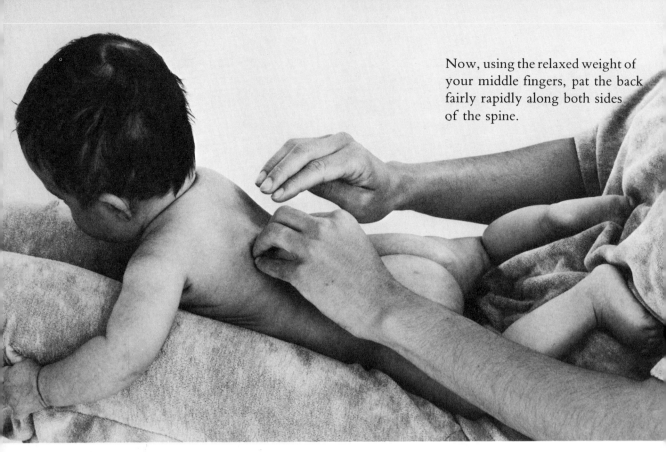

Now, using the relaxed weight of your middle fingers, pat the back fairly rapidly along both sides of the spine.

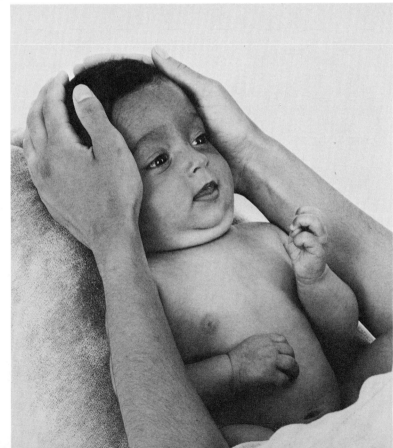

Finish by laying your baby on her back upon your thighs and gently placing your hands around her head.

Using a very light fingertip pressure, massage the top and sides of your baby's head.

BABY GYMNASTICS

From a few months of age on, your baby will begin making a conscious effort to try out various postures and kinds of movement. Sitting upright, crawling, standing, and walking are your infant's first major physical achievements, but before being able to attain upright postures and mobility, your baby must strengthen the active parts of his body. At this time a little prior knowledge and forethought on your part will do much to assist the even development of all the physical attributes that are your infant's natural birthright.

Every child is born supple, with flexible joints and the potential for a wide variety of movement. During the time it takes your baby to gain the strength necessary for standing and moving upright, your infant can be engaged in specific modes of play that make full use of the variety of movements his muscles and joints are intended to perform. In this way the young child strengthens flexible joints and maintains both a wider variety of movements and an even development of strength and suppleness.

By knowing the right exercises you can help your child to form a healthy, agile body that is strong and flexible, well balanced and coordinated.

A "SOFT" PHYSICAL EDUCATION

These exercises should be a learning experience for you and your infant. They provide you with a means of aiding your baby to explore and develop the boundaries of his movements, to discover what actions his body is designed to carry out and how far he can go. Every infant experiences minor falls in his efforts to stand on his own two feet. A relaxed body is unhurt by these impacts—it does not resist, it goes with them. and thus the shock of impact passes safely right through the body. The exercises outlined here encourage this kind of relaxation, and help your child to maintain relaxation in action. Knowing what exercises to apply to each part of the body gives you a way of keeping a check on the health and integrity of your infant's muscles and joints, and of ensuring that your child's movements remain unimpaired following minor injury.

Engaging your child in this type of activity creates a great source of satisfaction. Having satisfied his needs through the pleasure of movements and through physical contact—and your undivided attention—your child will be more relaxed and secure in his own company. Your growing insight into your child's physical capabilities will bring with it greater understanding and trust, which in turn will add to the security of your relationship. These exercises complement the development of your child perfectly because they allow your baby to maintain and improve his body's flexibility while it grows stronger. They will increase the pleasure and extend the boundaries of your recreation together, bringing to it a "soft" therapeutic dimension and a healthy purpose.

THE BENEFITS OF BALANCE

Maintaining the body's structural balance, the good posture which accompanies flexibility, is extremely beneficial as far as the healthy functioning of the internal organs and glands is concerned. Relaxed shoulders and an open chest greatly enhance respiration, and a relaxed abdomen greatly enhances digestion. The circulation of blood and lymphatic fluid, vital to the body's nourishment and defenses, increases with suppleness, and stamina—the means to persevere—is dependent on proper relaxation.

All this and more can be secured and maintained in your child through the early practice of a few simple exercises. Start with the most pleasurable exercise and slowly build on the routine, one exercise at a time. In this way they are easily learned, and the complete series can soon be included to maintain good posture and the health and integrity of all your infant's major muscles and joints. With your baby lying on your thighs, talk and sing to her; stroke and soothe your child while gently swaying your legs from side to side.

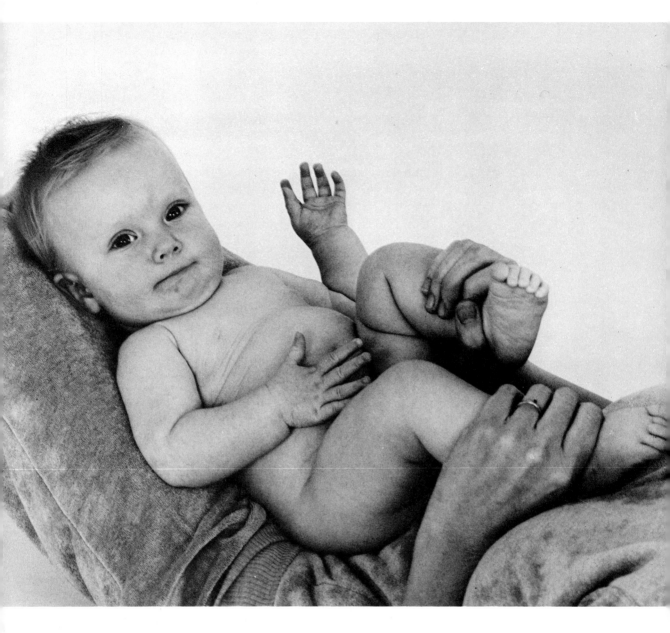

ANKLES, KNEES, AND HIPS

Now, holding your baby's legs from above the ankles, bend one leg as you semi-straighten the other.

Repeat playfully three or four times or more, to relax your baby's legs.

58

Now open the knees and bring the soles of the feet together.

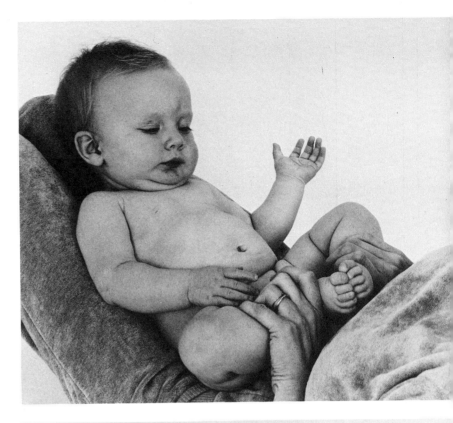

Now "clap" the feet together a few times in the same way as you would clap your hands, and if this is comfortable lift the feet to the abdomen, keeping the knees open.

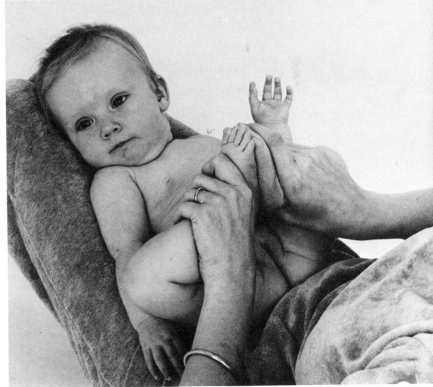

Clap the feet again, and if this is
comfortable lift the feet to the
chest, keeping the knees open.

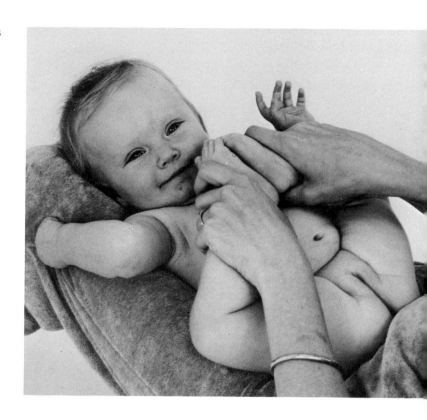

And then, if this is comfortable, to
the face, keeping the knees open.

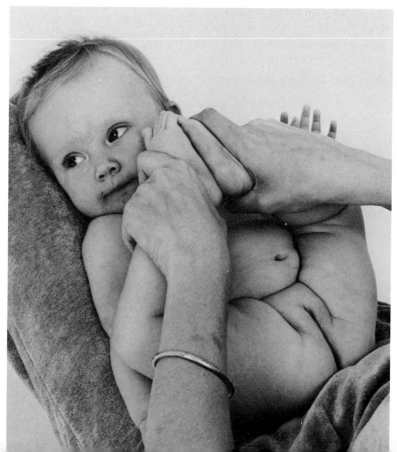

60

Now encourage your baby to
hold her foot.

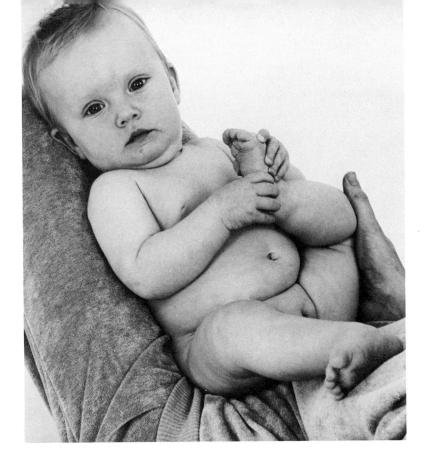

And then to lift her foot to he
mouth.

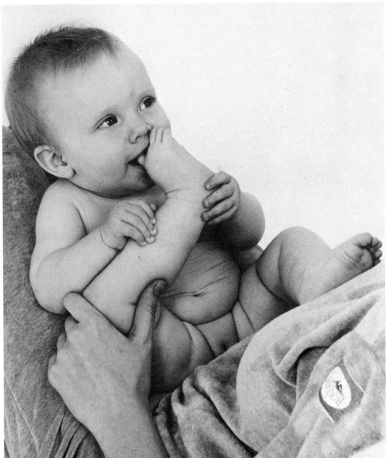

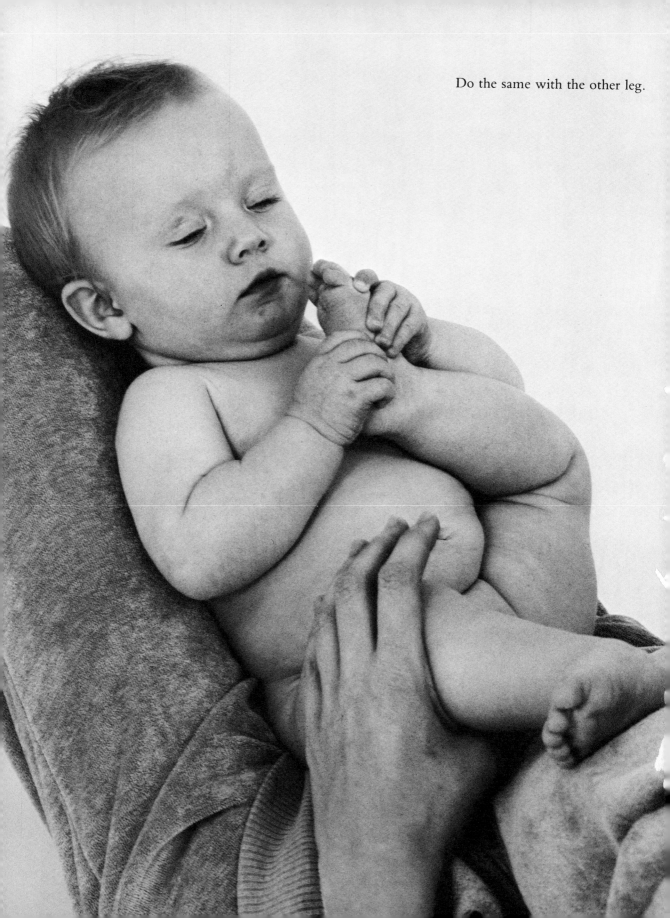

Do the same with the other leg.

When sitting with your child, try to make a habit of opening your baby's legs around your waist. If your baby resists, carry her on your hip, with her legs open around your side, before moving her to the front of your body.

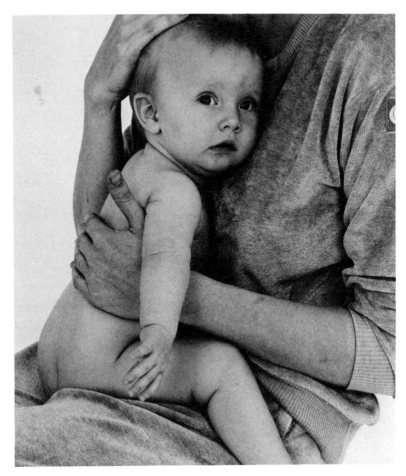

Open your baby's legs and feet.

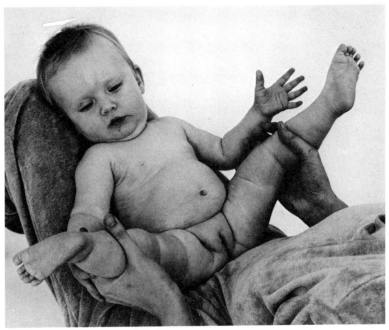

Now open the knees and bring the soles of the feet together. Lift your knees so that your baby is sitting upright with her back supported against your thighs.

If this is comfortable, encourage your baby to lean forward momentarily.

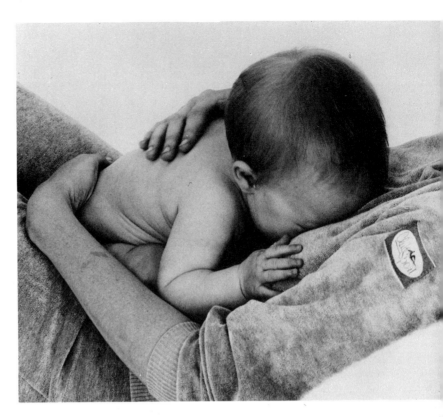

With your baby lying on her belly upon your thighs, gently press the instep of each foot to the buttocks.

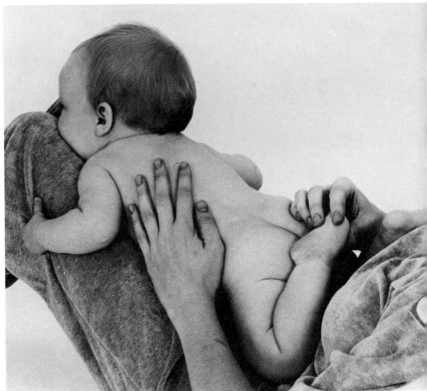

Now do this with both feet.

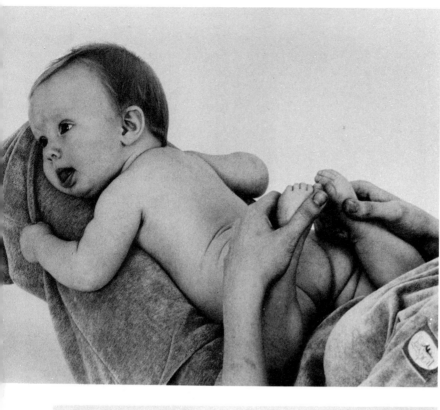

Now encourage your baby to sit back between her feet.

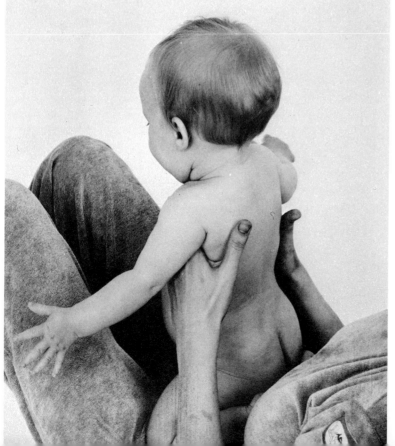

Or on her feet.

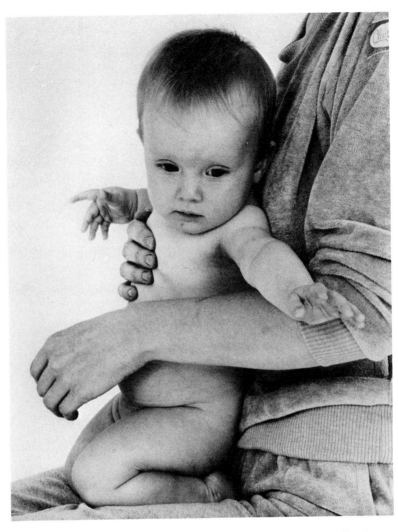

Each of these exercises should be practiced with a lot of affection. Make each exercise a loving game to be repeated as often as you both find pleasurable. These exercises will maintain and improve the flexibility and suppleness of your baby's legs and feet, and will encourage sitting positions.

ARMS AND SHOULDERS

With your baby lying back on your thighs, hold both hands and gently and playfully shake the arms, and as they relax bring them in line with the shoulders.

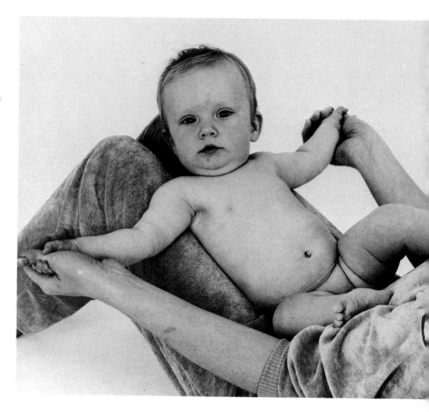

Now repeat and bring the arms in line with the ears.

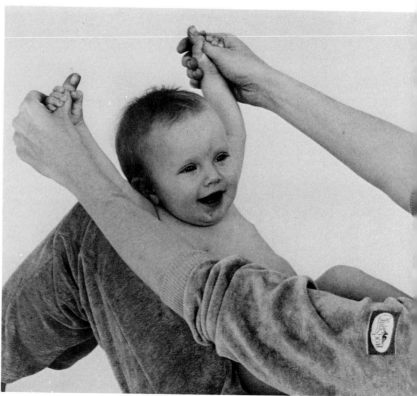

The first part of this exercise can also be frequently practiced with your baby sitting on your lap with her back to your abdomen. Open your baby's arms and "hug" them around your sides.

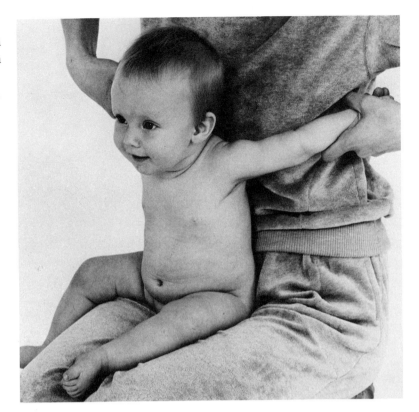

Or, when this is comfortable, with your baby lying on her belly upon your thighs, take both hands, open the arms and shake them gently.

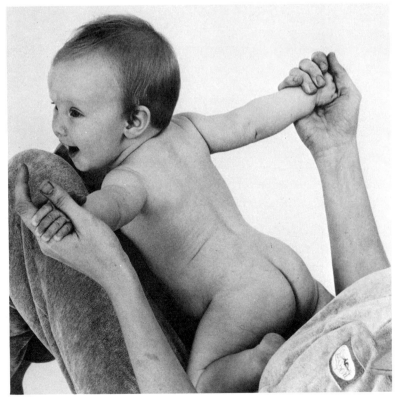

CHEST AND BELLY

Sitting with your legs straight in front of you, lay your baby on your legs with your knees just below the shoulder blades.

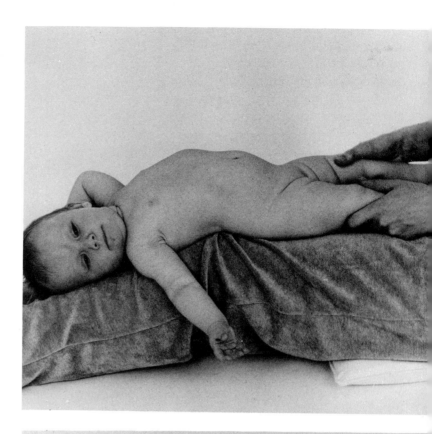

Now, keeping your baby's head and back in contact with your legs, gently lift your knees.

This exercise can be a lot of fun and highly therapeutic. Just bend and straighten your knees as quickly or as slowly as your baby finds enjoyable. If your baby lifts her head and breaks contact, stop the exercise and repeat it at another time.

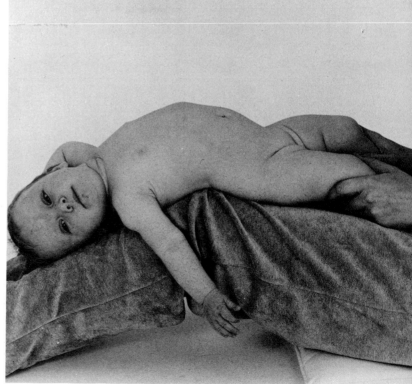

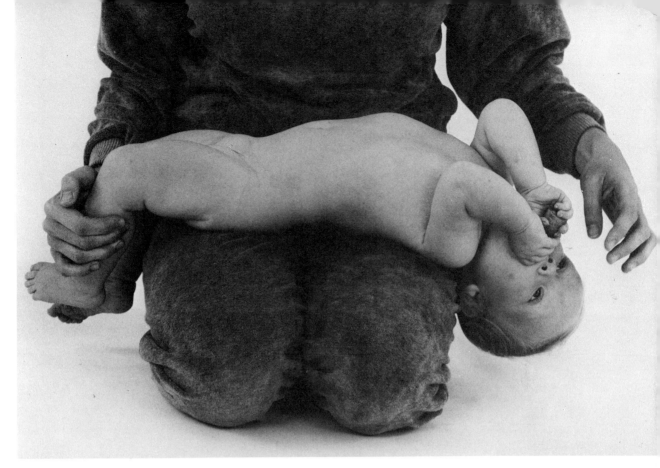

Sitting on your feet, lay your baby sideways across your thighs.

Rock your baby very gently, rolling your legs from side to side.

Now lay your baby back over your knees with the back of her head continuously in contact with your knees.

This position is ideal for massage of the chest and abdomen. All these positions help to increase the strength and flexibility of your baby's spine. The relaxation of the belly aids digestion, and the opening of the chest and shoulders, a deeper breathing rhythm.

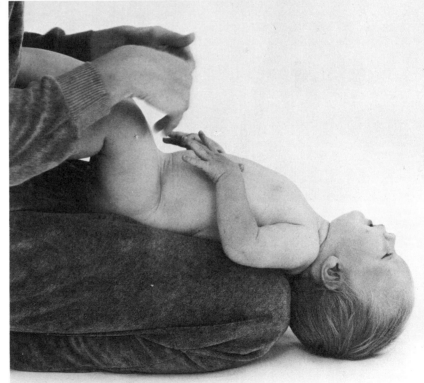

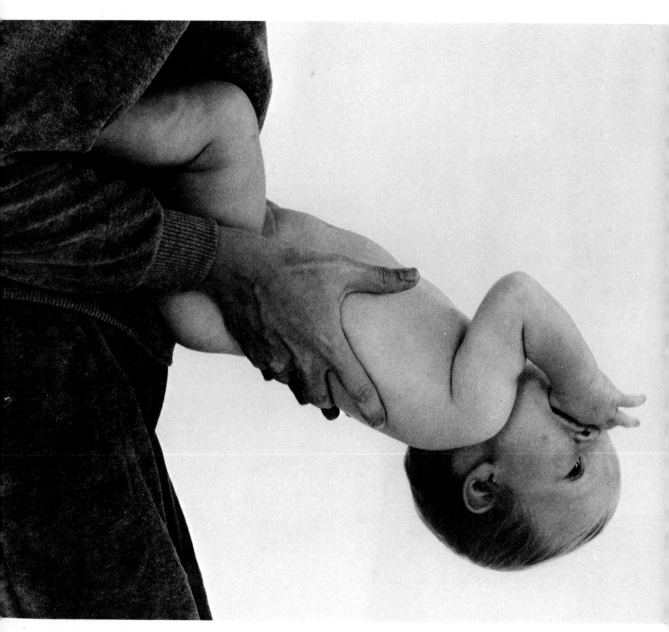

Backbending can also be
encouraged by opening your
baby's legs around your waist and
lifting your child while supporting
her upper spine from around the
shoulder blades.

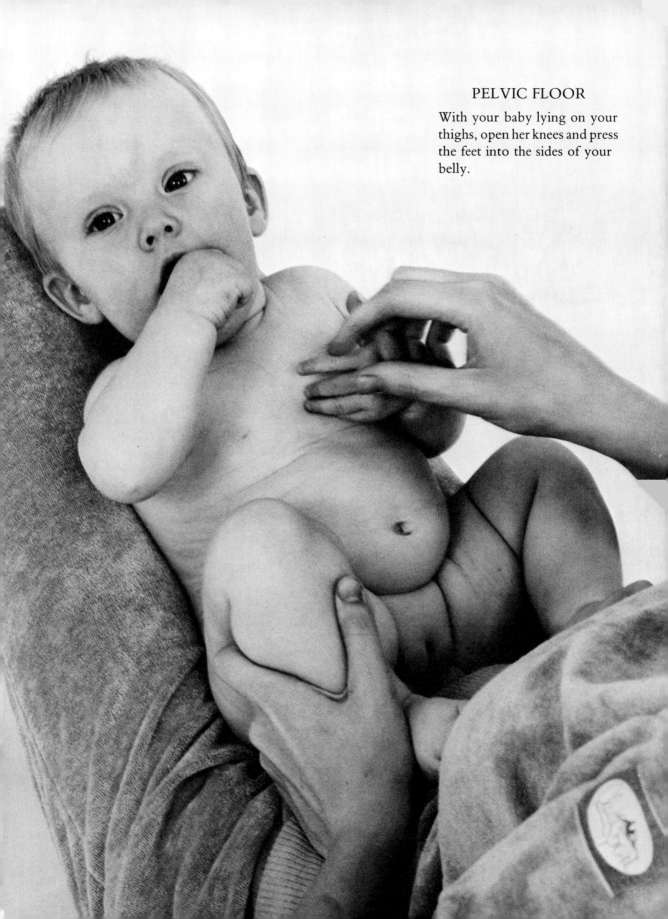

PELVIC FLOOR

With your baby lying on your thighs, open her knees and press the feet into the sides of your belly.

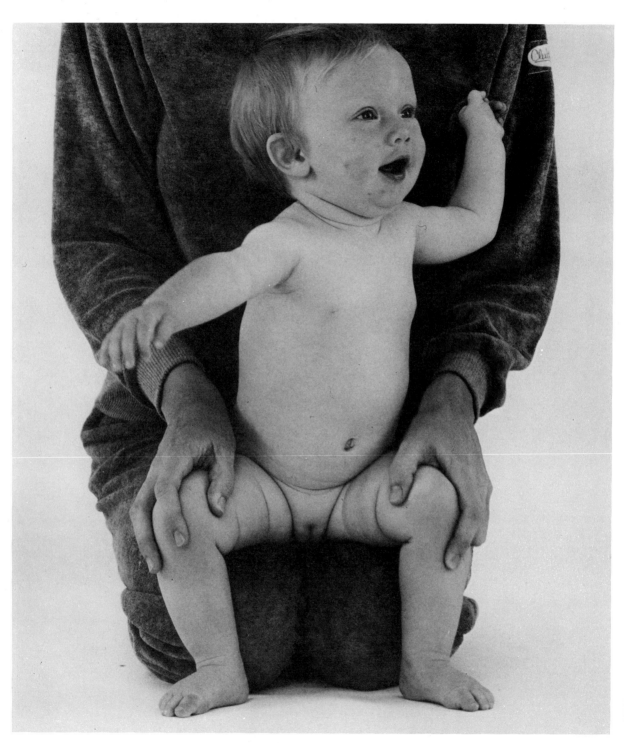

This can also be done with you
sitting on your feet and with your
baby sitting upright with her knees
open and her feet on the floor.

These exercises stretch and relax the pelvic-floor muscles and aid
the passing of solids and liquids, especially when practiced with
your baby in an upright position.

HEAD AND NECK

To maintain the flexibility of the neck as it grows stronger, sitting on your feet with your baby lying on your thighs, gently lift your baby onto her shoulders holding both legs from below the ankles. Kiss or blow on your baby's feet and maintain the position for about half a minute if pleasurable.

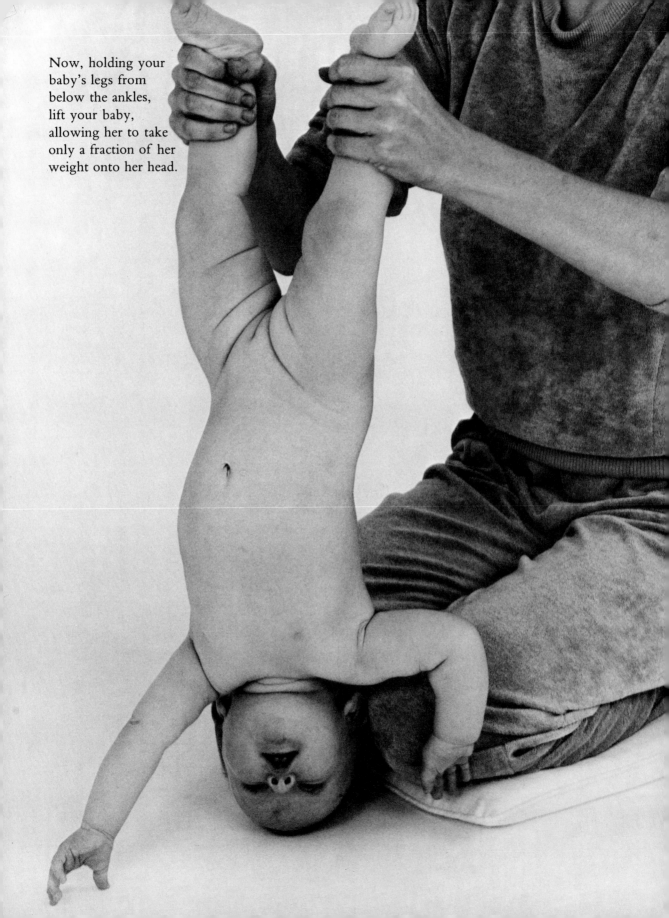

Now, holding your baby's legs from below the ankles, lift your baby, allowing her to take only a fraction of her weight onto her head.

DIGESTION AND RELAXATION

Many physicians seem to agree that parents all too often ascribe their baby's distress to disorders of their digestive system, namely gas or colic. They say that the need to be held, nurtured, and played with, that hunger, teething, and sometimes even illness are overlooked because gas and colic are convenient explanations. Most parents, however, agree that as a result of their babies' physical immaturity they do experience "gas" and sometimes colic, and that traditional methods of burping their babies bring relief.

A SOURCE OF CONTENTMENT

The abdomen or belly is recognized as a major emotional center. Anxiety, fear and excitement all emanate from this area, and such emotions provoke deep physiological changes that affect the baby's disposition and moods. For example, because of the baby's vulnerability, hunger can give rise to anxiety, loneliness, fear, and so on. Persistent abdominal tension also has a disruptive influence upon the body's structure as it pulls the chest and shoulders forward, rounds the upper back, and weakens the spine.

Some societies view the abdomen as a seat of wisdom and contentment. They maintain that when this area is properly relaxed, fears and anxieties are subdued and a blissful state pervades the whole body. Japanese children call this area *onaka,* meaning "the honored middle." According to their culture, proper relaxation of the abdomen brings tranquility and awareness, the ability to comprehend things with a clear mind.

DISCOMFORT AND REMEDY

Loving care and a relaxed parent can do a great deal to ensure that an infant feels calm and secure, but even a baby with the most tranquil of dispositions can, because of physical immaturity, experience abdominal tension and discomfort. Adults and children alike ingest air along with their intake of solids and liquids, and it is quite normal for there to be air in the stomach and intestines. However, the very young child often takes an uncomfortable amount of air into her stomach while feeding. Also because of the immaturity of a baby's digestive system, air in the intestines can sometimes result in an uncomfortable pocket of gas.

Correct positioning of your baby during and after feeding can help prevent excessive gas and provide relief. If your child is slouched or horizontal while feeding, air can accumulate in the stomach until it becomes considerably distended. The subsequent release of air tends to cause milk to be brought up. Keeping your baby's back reasonably straight during feeding, with the lower back supported upright, helps the baby to expel excessive air readily.

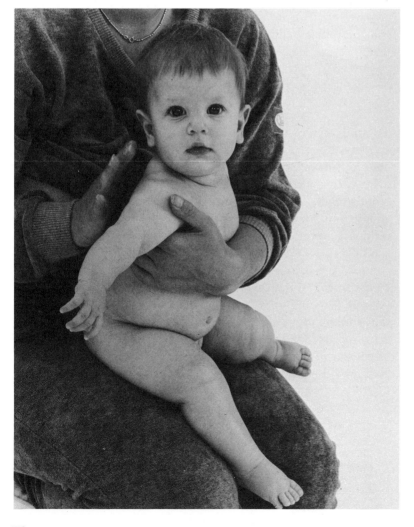

After a feeding you can help your baby to release "gas" as follows. Sitting with your child on your knees and with the baby leaning forward supported by one of your hands across the upper chest, stroke the baby's back from the base of the spine, upwards only. Then pat gently between the shoulder blades.

This can also be done with your baby lying across one shoulder. Some parents find this position more comfortable and more effective.

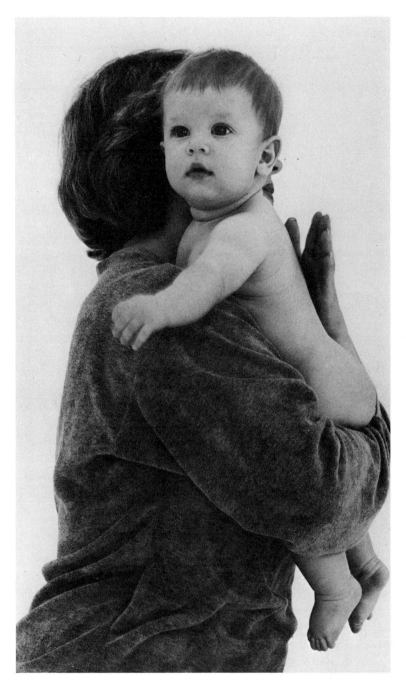

If you lay your baby down after a feed it is best to place her on her belly or right side. If the child is placed on her left side, any air in the stomach tends to pass into the intestine, which can cause discomfort.

Regular practice of the baby massage techniques and exercises given for the abdomen should help to maintain and improve her level of relaxation.

BREATHING AND
RELAXATION

Of all things necessary to life, to maintain and improve vitality and healthy functioning and development of the body, oxygen is perhaps the most important. "To breathe little is to feel little." "Inhibited breathing results in anxiety, apathy, loss of self-control, and loss of concentration." These are some of the conclusions of physical therapists and doctors, and modern medicine now recognizes physiotherapy as an invaluable part of the treatment of asthma and related disorders.

You will see that your child breathes with his lower chest and abdomen, which expand and contract in unison. This kind of breathing—abdominal breathing—is found only in children, good athletes, and healthy relaxed adults. It allows the base of the lungs, the diaphragm to descend into the abdomen. This has two major advantages as far as the healthy functioning of the body is concerned: first, it increases the volume of oxygen inhaled, and second, it massages the belly.

INTERNAL MASSAGE

With every inhalation the diaphragm descends, pushing the belly outwards as it gently presses its contents downwards. With each exhalation the diaphragm rises and, as it does so, creates a vacuum that draws the belly and its contents inwards. This movement greatly relaxes the internal organs and stimulates their function. It takes place some fifteen thousand times a day.

BREATHING AND FLEXIBILITY

The lungs are passive containers that are pulled into movement with the action of the rib cage. Their breathing capacity is dependent on the flexibility of the chest and on good posture, a straight back and open shoulders. When combined with a relaxed abdomen, this gives the maximum amount of oxygen for the least amount of effort.

RELIEVING CONGESTION

The young child always breathes through his nostrils, taking in air through the mouth only in an emergency, when the nostrils are congested. Because of this, minor respiratory disorders such as coughs and colds can prove a greater source of discomfort at night: they interfere with the child's natural rhythm of respiration and disturb his sleep.

With the change from wakefulness to sleep, the body relaxes and the breathing rhythm becomes deeper and slower. If at this time the baby's breathing is obstructed, the child usually awakens with a start. If this state of affairs continues, the baby becomes irritable and unhappy.

With your baby lying back supported upon your thighs, trace the outline of the cheekbones from the sides of the nose, pressing gently downwards and outwards with your index fingers. This helps to relieve congestion by opening the nostrils. (Try this on yourself first to make sure you have the correct technique.)

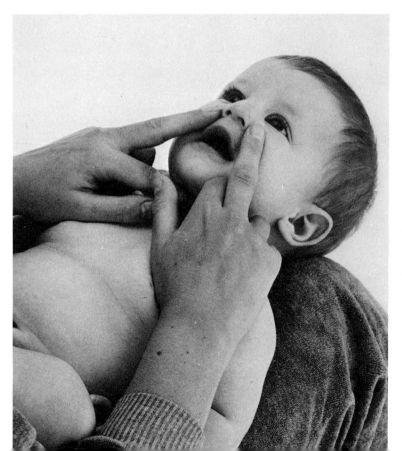

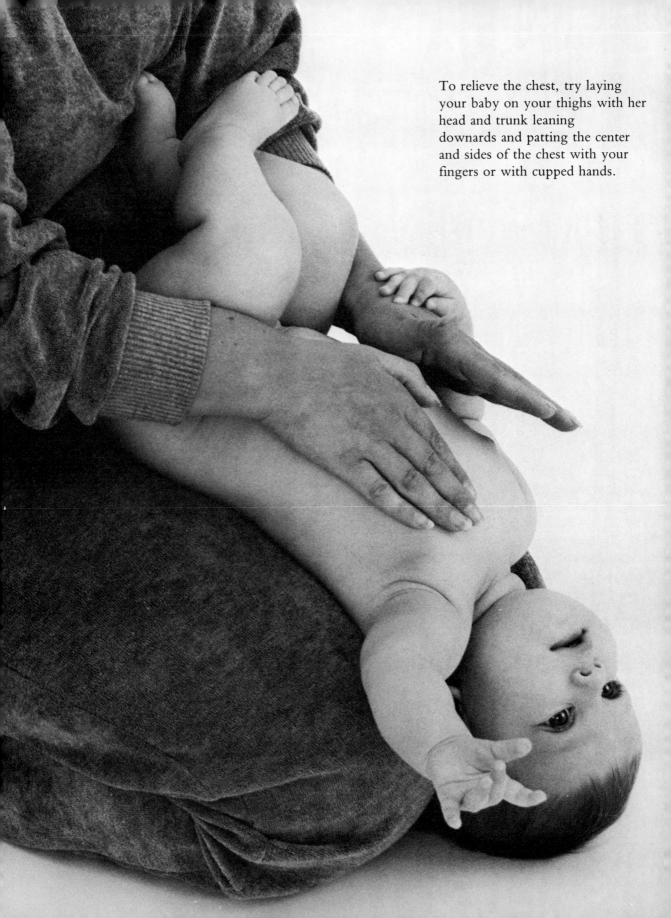

To relieve the chest, try laying your baby on your thighs with her head and trunk leaning downwards and patting the center and sides of the chest with your fingers or with cupped hands.

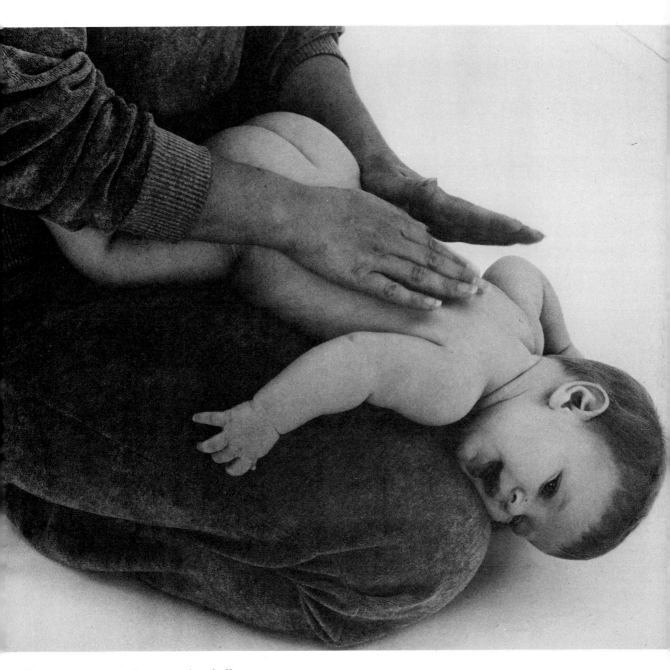

Now turn your baby on to her belly
and repeat across the upper back.

Place your baby in a more upright
position while sleeping by placing
something under the head of the
mattress. It is not safe to use
pillows or cushions in bed with
infants.

A chest and back massage given just before bedtime can be combined with the following technique to help relieve congestion and bring relief plus a good night's sleep.

The massage techniques given to relax the chest and belly, together with the exercises for the chest and abdomen, will do much to promote and maintain a regular rhythm of deep, relaxed breathing as your child develops.

GYMNASTICS FOR TODDLERS

From about fifteen months of age, or when your baby is standing and walking, the following routine practiced regularly once or twice a week will maintain your child's flexibility, good posture, and all the attributes associated with a relaxed, healthy body. This routine is a continuation of the baby routine adapted to suit your active child, and each series of exercises has been arranged in a sequence of development.

These exercises, practiced with love and affection, with lots of embraces, kisses, tickling, and so on, are extremely enjoyable and will provide a unique means for a heart-to-heart get-together with your child.

Start by practicing the first exercise from each sequence, and when your child is able to be rocked or comfortably played with in each one, move on to the second, and so on.

Be spontaneous: make each exercise a loving game and approach your child when you know she wants to play. Research over many years has shown that anxiety, fear, shock, and trauma go hand in hand with stiff muscles and joints. The frequent practice of this routine will ensure that from your child's first encounters with the disciplines of life, she will retain the ability to seek refuge in the pleasures of her movements, her capacity to raise her spirit through the good feelings that come with having and moving with a relaxed, flexible body.

LEGS AND FEET

These are the body's roots and the flexibility of their joints and the suppleness of their muscles are vital to the degree of ease with which the body stands and moves.

The flexibility of the hip joints is vital to the degree of ease with which we bend our body forward. By cultivating ease of movement in these joints we maintain the strength and integrity of the lower back and spine. The knees, together with the ankles, support the entire weight of the upright body. Consequently their flexibility is vital to the ease with which they transfer this moving weight to the ground.

BACKS OF THE LEGS
SERIES 1
With your infant lying back on your thighs, gently and playfully bring the feet to the sides of the head, allowing the knees to open.

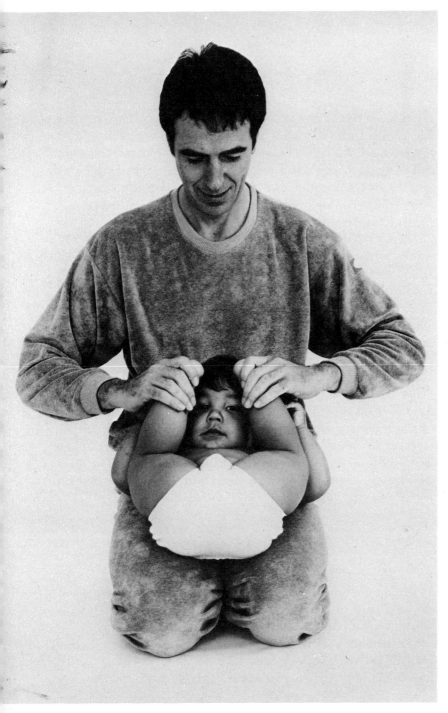

When it is comfortable to do so, this exercise can also be practiced on the floor.

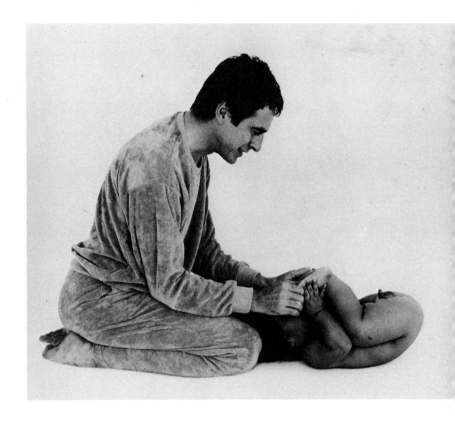

When this is comfortable, help your child to perform a backward roll.

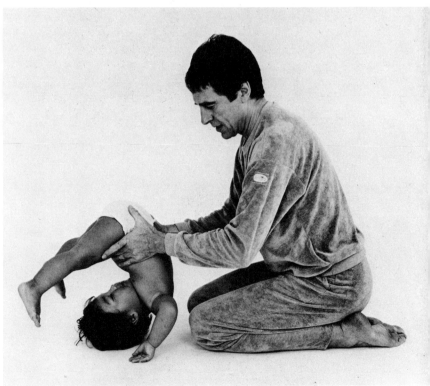

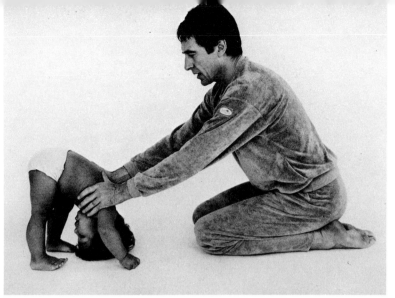

And encourage your infant to stand leaning forward with straight legs.

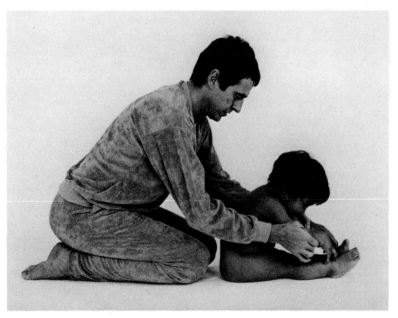

Encourage your child to sit with straight legs. (Pull the buttocks outwards to make sure your child sits on the backs of the legs).

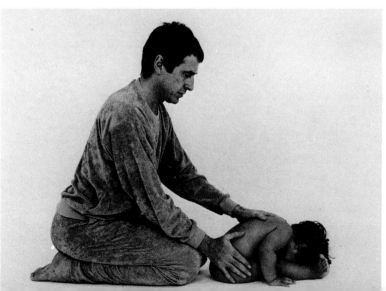

When this is comfortable, encourage leaning forward onto the shins.

INSIDES OF THE LEGS
SERIES 2
With your infant lying back on your thighs, open the legs and feet.

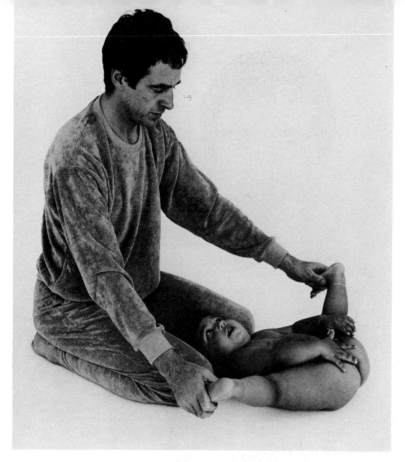

When it is comfortable to do so, this exercise can also be practiced on the floor.

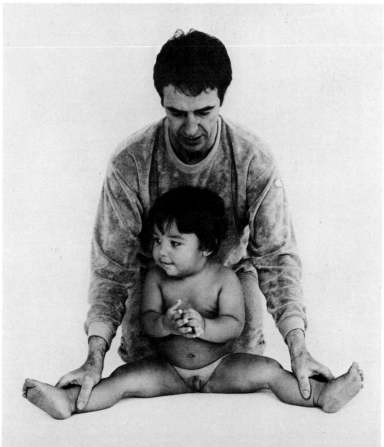

When this is comfortable encourage your child to sit with open legs (on the backs of the legs, not on the buttocks).

When this is comfortable,
encourage your child to lie
forward in this position.

FRONTS OF THE LEGS
SERIES 3

Encourage your child to sit
between his feet, on the backs of
his legs, with both feet turned
inwards.

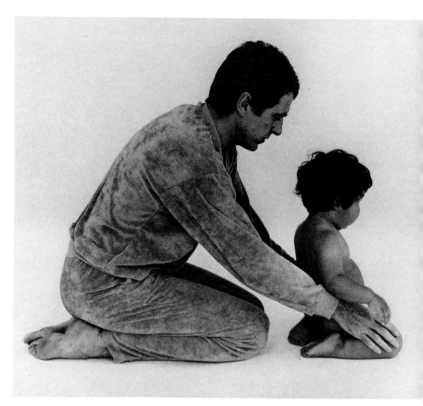

When this is comfortable,
encourage your child to lie back
upon your thighs.

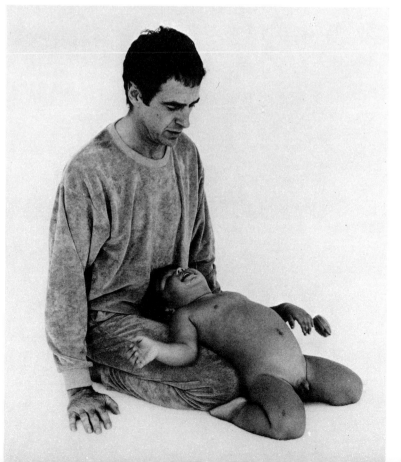

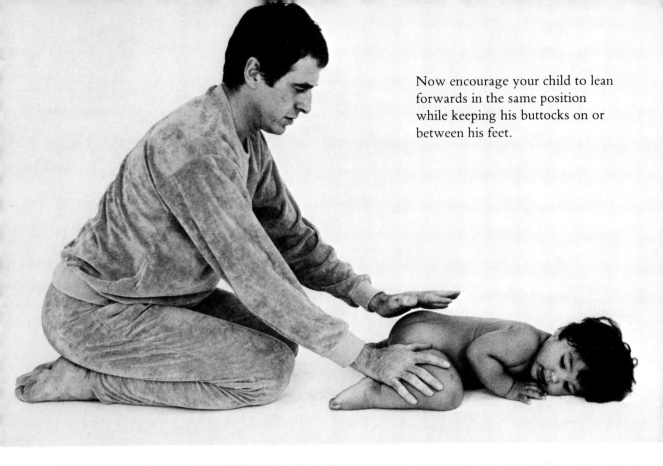

Now encourage your child to lean
forwards in the same position
while keeping his buttocks on or
between his feet.

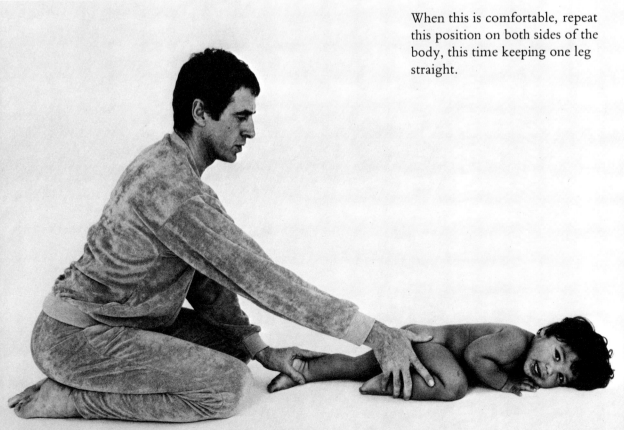

When this is comfortable, repeat
this position on both sides of the
body, this time keeping one leg
straight.

A perfect posture.

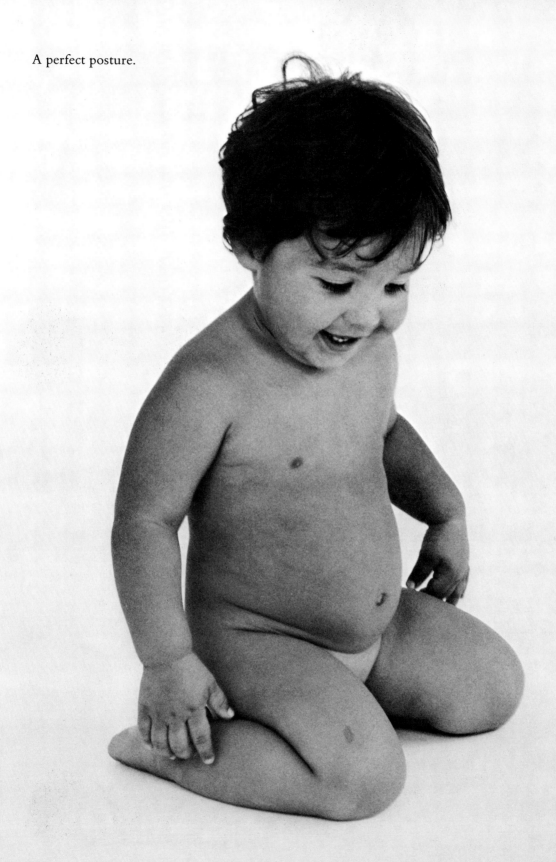

PELVIC FLOOR

Every mother knows how important it is to relax these muscles during childbirth; and every solid or liquid which is passed through the base of the abdomen calls for the relaxation of the pelvic-floor muscles.

The following exercises will maintain and improve the relaxation of the pelvic floor and lower abdomen, the flexibility of the hip joints and the strength of the lower back.

SERIES 4
Encourage your child to sit on the back of his legs with knees open and feet together.

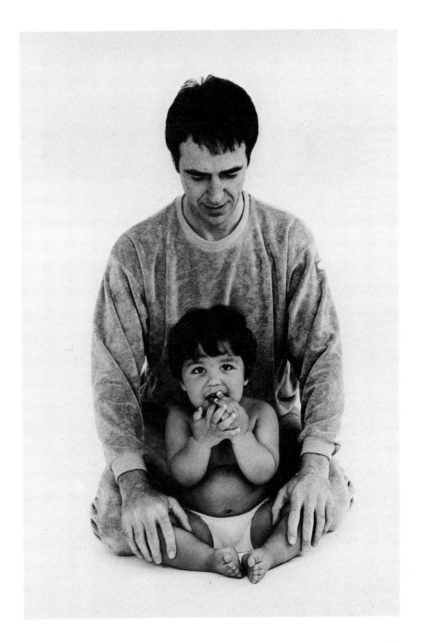

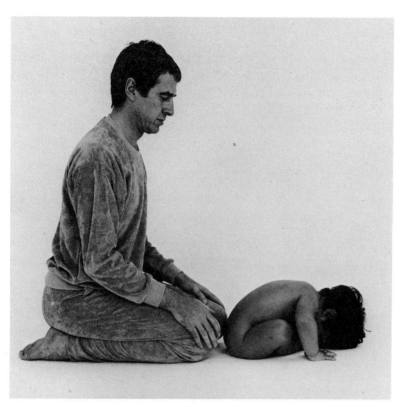

When this is comfortable, encourage your child to lean forward.

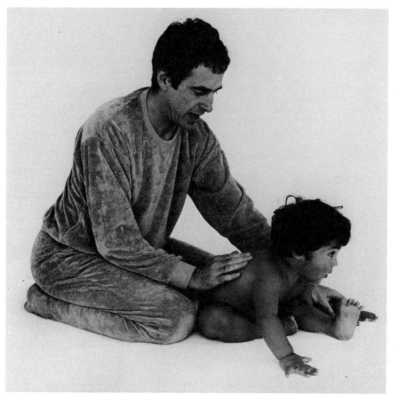

Now encourage your child to lean forward with one leg straight. Repeat for both sides.

A perfect posture.

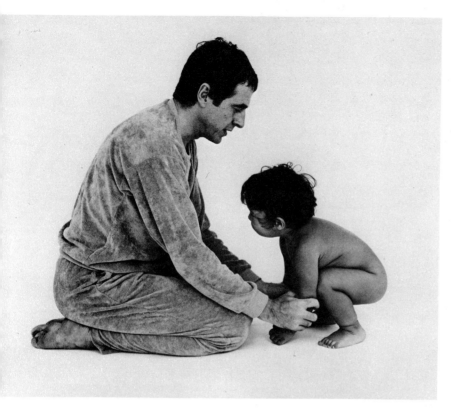

Encourage your child to squat

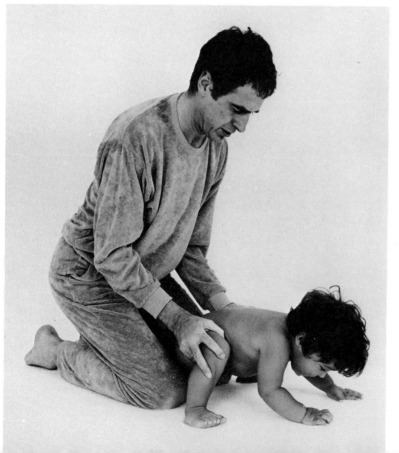

Encourage your child to lean
forward while squatting.

BACKBONE

Known as "Shiva's wand" and "Kali's vine," the backbone supports and protects parts of the body's nervous system, a tree of life that is responsible for all mental and physical activity. From each joint in the spine root, nerves project and multiply to serve every living part of the body. The flexibility of the spine is crucial to the integrity of these nerves, to the flexibility of the chest and its breathing capacity, and to the relaxation of the abdomen and ease of digestion.

The following exercises are a *progression*. With each series, make sure that the first stage is comfortable for your child before moving on to the next.

HEAD AND NECK

SERIES 5

Keeping your child facing you, his head in line with his body, lift and support his back on your thighs, and encourage him to stand on his shoulders.

When this is comfortable, keep
the face forward and lift your child
on to his neck and shoulders while
holding his legs.

When this is comfortable, keep the face forward and encourage your child to take his legs back over his head.

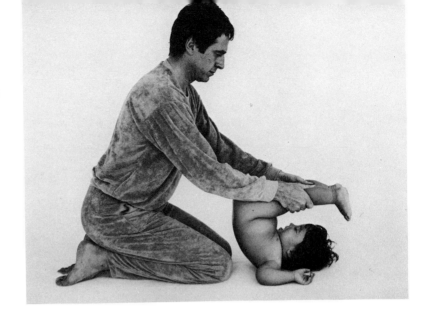

When this is comfortable, keep the face forward and gently encourage your child to take his feet over his head, by degrees, until touching the floor momentarily.

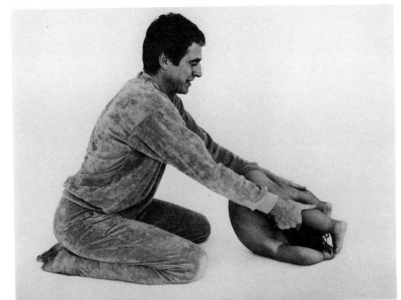

Firmly holding both sides of your child's head, relax the spinal muscles by gently pulling and releasing, rocking the entire body backwards and forwards.

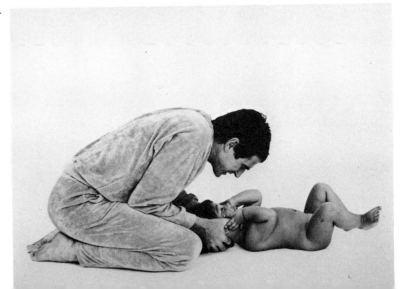

Encourage your child to stand on
his head while supporting his
weight from the waist.

When this is comfortable,
encourage your child to stand on
his head while you support his
weight from below the ankles.

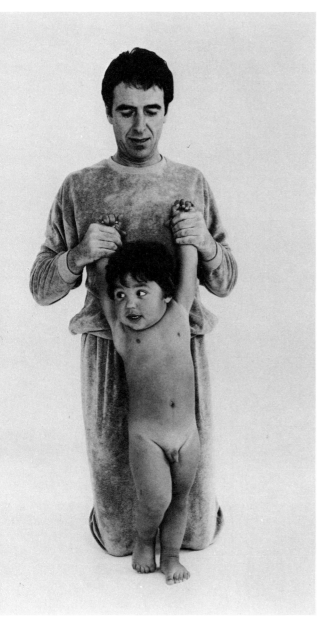

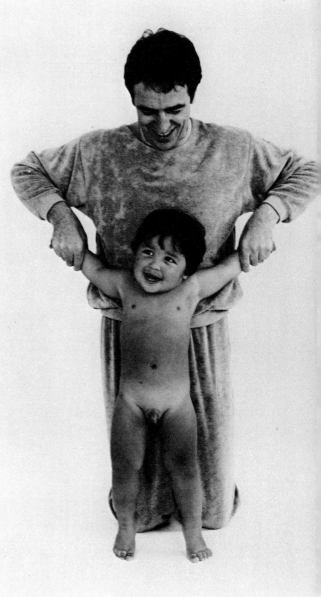

CHEST AND SHOULDERS
SERIES 6
Holding your child firmly from
each forearm below the wrist,
encourage the child to lift his
arms in line with his ears and
shoulders, keeping his feet on the
floor.

Now encourage your child to
open his arms in line with his
shoulders, keeping his feet on
the floor.

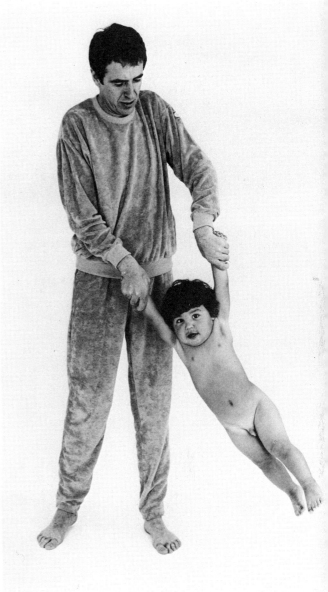

When this is comfortable, open the arms and shoulders and gently press the upper back forward with your thigh, keeping the child's feet on the floor.

When this is comfortable, gently swing your child once or twice from side to side holding both forearms firmly from below the wrist.

Now encourage your child to stand on his hands. Keep the body tilted as shown to allow the child to lift his head clear of the floor, and hold firmly from the lower legs below the ankles.

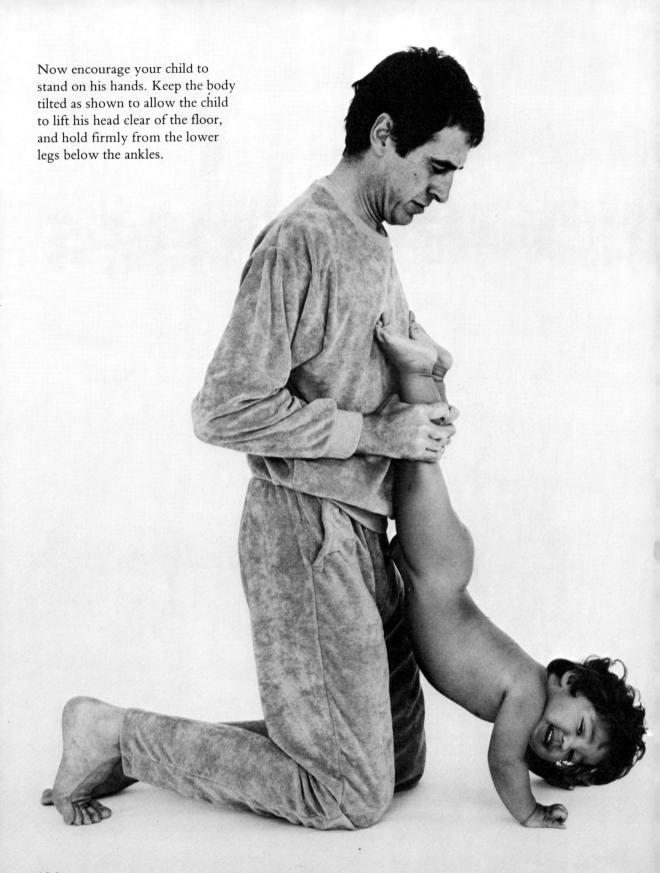

The test of a healthy, flexible backbone is the ability to perform a backbend. This can be greatly encouraged by practicing the following sequence of exercises.

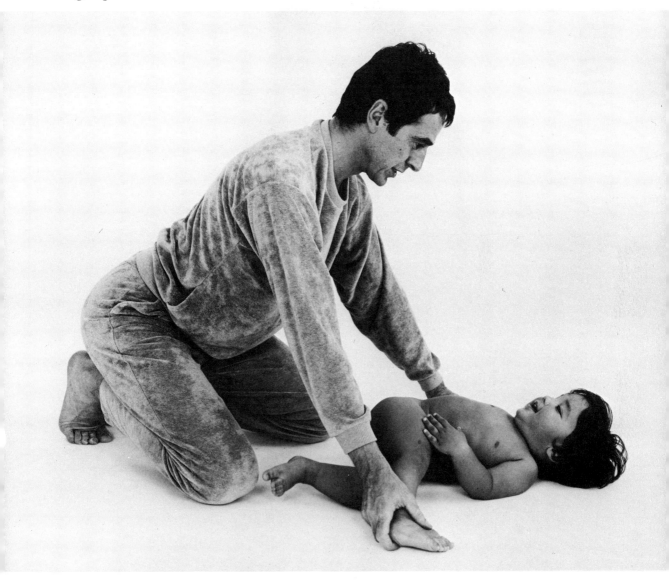

BACKBONE

SERIES 7

First relax your child by holding his right hand on the floor with the right arm extended sideways and gently rolling the right hip and leg in the opposite direction.
Repeat both sides.

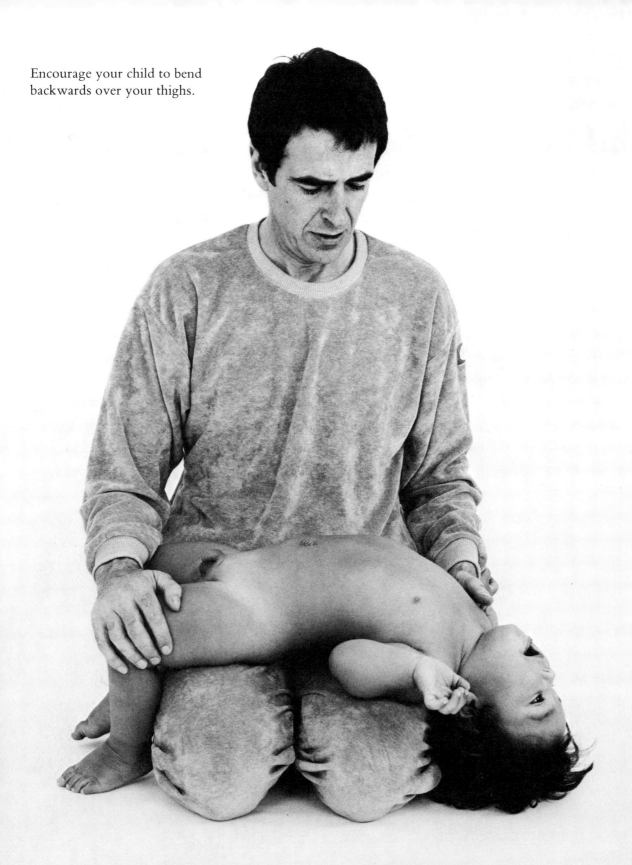

Encourage your child to bend
backwards over your thighs.

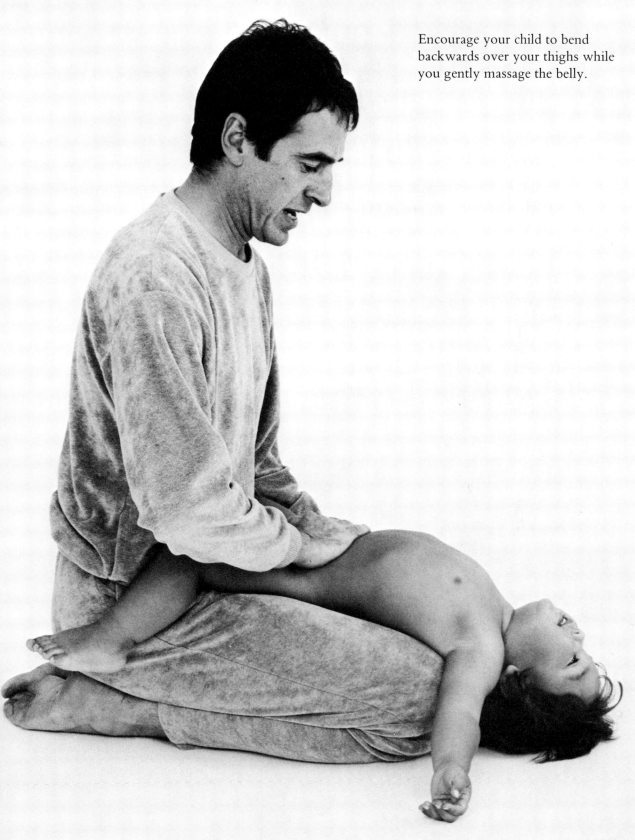

Encourage your child to bend
backwards over your thighs while
you gently massage the belly.

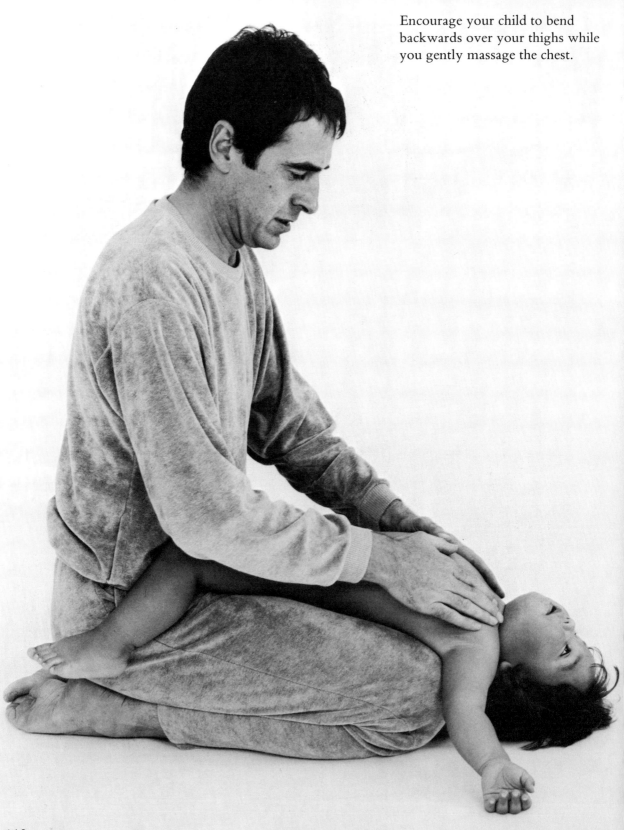

Encourage your child to bend backwards over your thighs while you gently massage the chest.

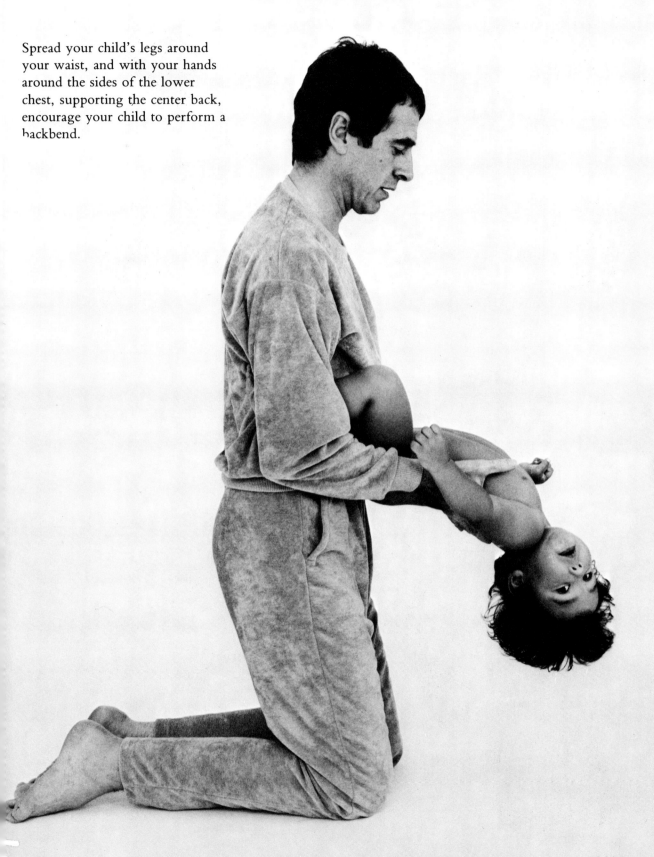

Spread your child's legs around your waist, and with your hands around the sides of the lower chest, supporting the center back, encourage your child to perform a backbend.

Lying on the floor, bend your
knees and encourage your child
to lean back against your legs by
gently extending both arms,
holding from below the wrists.

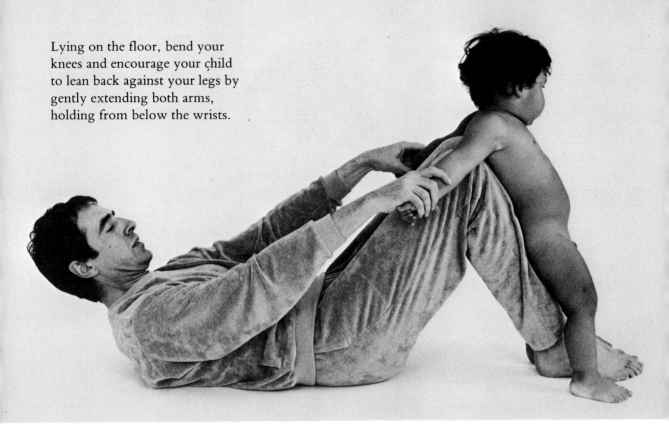

Now lift your legs, and holding
your child from the hips
encourage him to bend his
upper back over your knees.

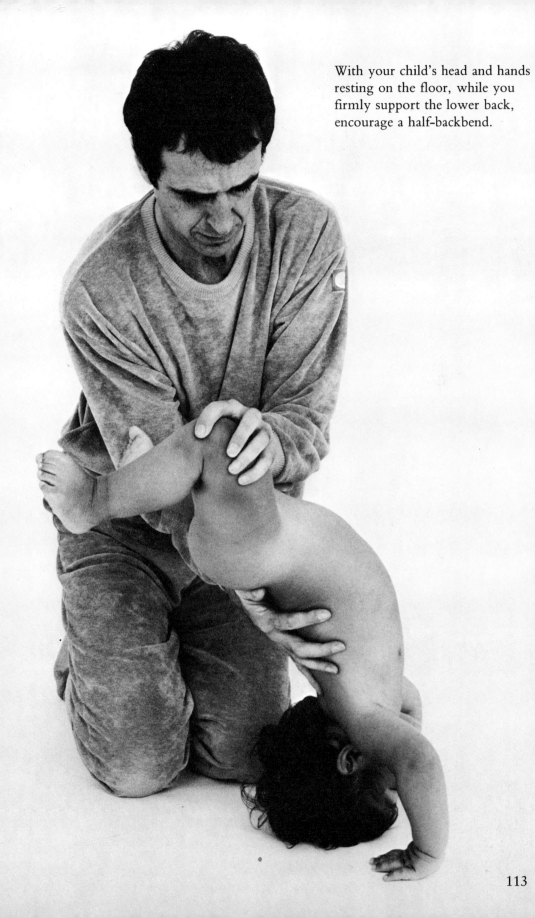

With your child's head and hands resting on the floor, while you firmly support the lower back, encourage a half-backbend.

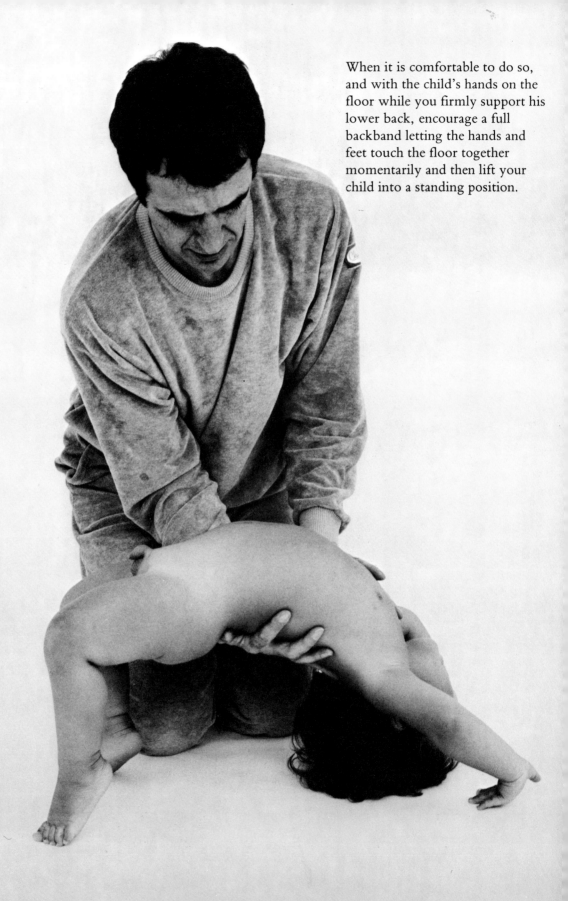

When it is comfortable to do so, and with the child's hands on the floor while you firmly support his lower back, encourage a full backband letting the hands and feet touch the floor together momentarily and then lift your child into a standing position.

114

Peter Walker lives in London, where he has conducted
workshops on postnatal exercise, stretching, and baby massage.